∞

Heroes of God

Henri Daniel-Rops

Heroes of God

Eleven Courageous Men and Women Who Risked Everything to Spread the Catholic Faith

SOPHIA INSTITUTE PRESS®
Manchester, New Hampshire

Heroes of God: Eleven Courageous Men and Women Who Risked Everything to Spread the Catholic Faith is an English translation of *Aventuriers de Dieu* that was previously published in English by Hawthorn Books, Inc., New York, in 1959 under the title *The Heroes of God*. This 2002 edition by Sophia Institute Press includes minor editorial revisions to the original text.

Sophia Institute Press®
Box 5284, Manchester, NH 03108
1-800-888-9344
www.sophiainstitute.com

Nihil obstat: John A. Goodwine, J.C.D., *Censor Librorum*
Imprimatur: Francis Cardinal Spellman, Archbishop of New York
Yonkers, December 22, 1958

Library of Congress Cataloging-in-Publication Data

Daniel-Rops, Henri, 1901-1965.
  [Aventuriers de Dieu. English]
  Heroes of God : eleven courageous men and women who risked
    everything to spread the Catholic faith / Henri Daniel-Rops.
    p. cm.
  ISBN 1-928832-62-8 (pbk. : alk. paper)
  1. Missionaries — Biography. I. Title.
  BV3700 .D2313 2002
  266'.2'0922 — dc21   2002007230

02 03 04 05 06 07 10 9 8 7 6 5 4 3 2 1

∞

Contents

∞

∞

Foreword

So many splendid figures have written pages in the history of Christian missions during the past two thousand years that it is difficult to choose among them. In all ages, in all countries, men and women have devoted body and soul to the task of making the Gospel known in those parts of the world still in the dark. Each one of these spokesmen for Christ, these Adventurers of God, had his own special plan of action, each his own special crises, too often his own special tragedy. From this infinite variety, here are eleven examples; others just as fine might have been chosen.

In bearing witness to these noble figures, may the following pages remind us that all these heroes had one and the same design. All of them lived, all of them suffered, all of them died to hasten the fulfillment — as much as it is possible for it to be fulfilled on earth — of the wish that every Christian addresses to the Father: "Thy kingdom come."

H.D.-R.

∞

Heroes of God

St. Paul

∞

The First Missionary

It was the year 36 of our era. Six years had gone by since that April day when anyone passing a certain bare knoll at the gates of Jerusalem could look up to see a so-called prophet who claimed to be "the Son of God," nailed to the Cross of infamy and dying between two scoundrels. Despite this devastating blow to the spread of His doctrines, however, the zealous followers of the Man called Jesus were not at all discouraged. Not only did their movement continue to flourish in the Holy City, but it spread, putting down roots in many corners of Palestine, winning initiates in ever-growing numbers. Hadn't these people been broadcasting the story that their Master — what a piteous Master! — had conquered death, had been resurrected, and for forty days thereafter had appeared to many of His faithful followers, and even that — what sheer impudence! — after His Ascension into Heaven, He had sent down the Holy Spirit to guide and encourage His people?

That was enough. The leaders of the Jewish people and the princes of the priesthood decided to take action. And that is

why, on this historic morning of the year 36, we might have
seen a howling mob dragging a young man across one of the
empty fields just outside the city walls. The victim of the
mob's torture was a solemn youth with shining brow, who
prayed as he let himself be pushed and jostled by the crowd.
His name resounded above the hostile cries. "Death to Stephen! Death to the blasphemer!" Had not Stephen had the
audacity to declare before the entire Sanhedrin that this Jesus
who was crucified on Calvary was indeed the true Messiah,
and that the whole lot of them — priests, doctors, elders all —
would come to judgment bearing the onus of deicide? Nothing
short of lapidation could properly punish such sacrilegious
words. So stones must fly and heavy blocks must crash down
upon the young victim who, although bleeding and gasping
for breath, begged the Lord's pardon for his executioners.[1]

Watching this scene with eyes like coals was a lean, red-
haired lad with tensely clamped jaws. His somber attire, the
long curls that hung from his temples, and the string of many
little boxes hanging around his neck (each containing a verse
of the Bible written on a strip of parchment) proclaimed him
to be a student of the religious sciences, the disciple of some
rabbi, a future Doctor of the Law. Seeing that some of the executioners had made themselves more comfortable by taking
off their tunics, he said, "Give them to me. I will keep them for
you." As a man of God, he had no wish to stain his hands with

---

[1] Acts 7:59. Scripture quotations throughout are from *The
Holy Bible in the St. Peters' Edition* (Westminster Version),
published by Hawthorn Books, Inc., New York.

the blood of Stephen, but as a pious Jew, he shared the senti-
ments of the turbulent mob, including its hatred of the Galilean
and his group. In his manner, he was helping the execution.

His name was Saul. He was the son of a well-to-do merchant of Tarsus in Cilicia, a region adjoining Syria. Its many
colonies of Jews who had settled in all the cities had more or
less taken over the business and trade of Cilicia. Saul was not
a handsome fellow, being of medium height, bow-legged, pre-
maturely bald, and with eyebrows that were too thick. But
those who noted his mobile features, his premature wrinkles,
and his deep-set eyes must inevitably have felt that here was a
profound intelligence destined for great things. To see him was
to sense his passion for ideas, the violence of his feelings, his
raging thirst for the Absolute.

His parents were Pharisees. Zealots and strict observers of
the letter of the Law, they had taught him that nothing on
earth was more important than living in accordance with the
Divine Word, and that the Lord was paramount. It was therefore quite natural that Saul, brought up as he was, should hate
the Prophet of Galilee and His crew. When he had arrived in
Jerusalem shortly after the liquidation of the Jesus matter, his
teachers had assured him that the death sentence of the false
Messiah was quite warranted by His blasphemies, by His revolt
against the precepts of the Law, and by His claim to speak for
the Father. Stephen was a disciple of the Christ: let him die!

And yet Saul could not wipe the frightful scene of torture
from his memory. Night after night, he was haunted by the
victim's face — his victim — so peaceful under the vicious
rain of deadly stones. He could not help admiring the calm

with which Stephen uttered his last words, asking God's absolution for his tormentors, words that echoed in his heart
with tones of reproach. When he was alone at night, a sickness
of the soul came over Saul, a feeling he could not throw off.
He repeated to himself the words of Jesus, even though they
caused him great uneasiness. Had not the Prophet of Galilee
denounced the violent, the proud, the smug of mind, the hard
of heart? And did not any or all of these apply to Saul?

No, no! He must not give way to such unhealthy scruples.
The Law is the Law. He who violates it must perish; he who
follows it is with God. To hate Jesus and track down the people
of His sect: such was his true duty.

There were rumors in Jerusalem that the faithful followers
of the so-called Messiah had established a stronghold at Damascus in Syria. "I will go there," declared Saul to the High
Priest. And he departed, armed with official authorization, determined to give no quarter.

During the week in which he followed the sandy track to
the north, a strange frenzy seized him, as though his mission
to chastise the disciples of the Christ were necessary to prove
to himself that he was in the right. One fine August day at
about noon, he was approaching the palms and plane trees of
an oasis, admiring the everlasting snows that crowned Mount
Hermon, silhouetted in white against the spotless blue of the
sky, when suddenly a great light flashed down from heaven
and enveloped him. As the traveler fell to the ground, he
heard a voice saying, "Saul, Saul, why dost thou persecute
me?" He stammered, "Who art Thou, Lord?" The voice replied, "I am Jesus, whom thou dost persecute." Overwhelmed

and trembling, the man murmured, "What wilt Thou have me do?" And the answer came: "Arise and go into the city, and it shall be told thee what thou must do."[2]

Saul got up, staggering. Total darkness had succeeded the brilliant sunshine. Although his eyes were wide open, he could see nothing. His traveling companions stared at him in silent astonishment. They had seen him fall, and they had heard confused sounds of voices without distinguishing words. What was the meaning of this mysterious incident?

Saul himself had understood — and forever. He knew now that the object of his hate and his pursuit was indeed the Messiah, the Son of God. As he lay gasping on the sandy road, he felt himself in the hands of the Power whom no one could resist. The instant the miraculous darkness broke over him, he realized what his restless soul had so long been seeking without knowing it. Henceforth there would never be enough days in his life to bear witness to his love of Him who had chosen him among all men to be His spokesman, of this Jesus, who had loved him enough to strike straight to his heart.

Thus summoned to His service by Jesus Himself, what leading role would Saul be called upon to play? To answer sincere doubts and legitimate suspicions, it would appear that Christ Himself had decided miraculously to transform an implacable adversary into a fervent servitor. The blinded traveler resumed his journey. Obedient to his orders, he entered the city and

[2] Acts 9:4-7.

took up residence with a Jewish shopkeeper named Judas. Or rather, he went into hiding there, bewildered, speechless, refusing food and drink. For several days, he remained thus prostrated, meditating on his error and on its just punishment.

Then, suddenly, a friendly voice sounded in his ears. A disciple of the Galilean came to his side and spoke kindly to him. It was Ananias, one of the members of the Christian community in Damascus, a wise and good man. Christ had appeared to him and had said, "Arise and go into the street which is called Straight, and seek in the house of Judas one Saul, from Tarsus . . . and lay hands upon him that he might see." Stunned by such an order, Ananias had dared reply, "Lord, I have heard from many of this man and of all the evil he hath done to Thy saints in Jerusalem." To which the Lord said, "Go, for this man is a vessel chosen by me."[3]

The vessel, the instrument of Christ: that was to be the sole object of Saul's life from that moment on. To serve His glory, to spread His word, to make known His deeds and example: he would know no other purpose. Restored to the light by Ananias, he had but one desire: to prepare himself for the new task ahead. First, he spent long months of retreat in the middle of the desert — just as Jesus Himself had done before He began to speak — meditating upon himself, gathering his strength, delving deeply into the doctrines of Him who henceforth would be his only Master.

Then he returned to Damascus. Was it not here that he should first appear as a faithful follower of Christ, since it was

---

[3] Acts 9:11-15.

to this city that he had planned to come as an enemy? In the public marketplaces and in the synagogues of the Jews, Saul proclaimed his new Faith. The general astonishment was profound. People asked each other whether this could be the same Saul who used to persecute anyone evoking the name of Jesus.

By merely describing his personal experience, the new convert won many new souls to Christ — so many, in fact, that the local Jews, disturbed and angry, plotted an ambush that would silence the renegade forever. As a result, Saul was forced to flee Damascus. And, since the gates were guarded, his friends hid him in a big fish basket and lowered him from the city walls. It was an admission on the part of the enemies of the Christ that Saul was a man to fear.

Returning to Jerusalem from Damascus, Saul considered placing all his youthful energy, his courage, and his devotion at the disposition of the Apostles, but his offer was received with great suspicion. The faithful of the Holy City still remembered Saul as a violent, fanatical rabbinical student who hated the very name of Jesus. The story of the miracle that he had experienced was greeted with almost general skepticism. Luckily, one of the most respected of the leaders of the young Church, the venerable Barnabas, was favorably impressed with Saul and took him under his wing.

So Saul served his apprenticeship with the wise old man, who took him to Antioch with him. Here Saul worked for two years with Barnabas, teaching the doctrines of Jesus, evoking the earthly appearance of the Lord, His death and Resurrection. During this period, he continued to nurture his inner life, praying much, fasting, and increasing his self-denials. And Jesus, who had not deserted the man He Himself had chosen, continued to maintain His mystical relationship with Saul. It was at Antioch, without doubt, that Saul experienced the mysterious visions that he was later to describe to his friends in Corinth, where, in divine ecstasy, he had revealed to him a few of the secrets of God.

He had now attained maturity. He understood perfectly the rule that the Christ had assigned to him. Before He ascended into Heaven to take His seat at the right hand of God, had not Jesus said to His followers, "Go ye, therefore, make disciples of all the nations, baptizing them in the name of the Father and of the Son and of the Holy Spirit, teaching them to observe all that I have commanded you"?[4]

Saul obeyed literally this supreme order of the Lord. He set off to cross and recross the wide world as it was then known, wherever he could, wherever there might be souls to win to the Christ. The vocation of missionary, today as two thousand years ago, pushes ardent souls to sacrifice the joys of life to the thankless (although admirable) task of teaching the catechism to unbelievers or of carrying the consolation of Christ to the suffering.

Although a major decision of this kind today seems perfectly in line with Christianity, it was in considerable question when it was made by Saul. The first followers of Jesus were of Jewish blood and faith. They were pious devotees of the Holy Law as it was handed down to mankind by Abraham, Moses,

[4] Matt. 28:19-20.

and the prophets. They might well ask whether the exact design of the Christ was indeed that His doctrine should be revealed to all peoples, even the pagans, or whether it should be reserved for the elect of the children of Israel. In other words, were the Christians a community of Jews who had recognized Jesus as the awaited Messiah? Or were they a new people, including both pagans and Jews, who had received the baptism of penitence, who believed in Jesus as God become man, and who lived according to the precepts of love?

The answer, for anyone who has seriously considered the teachings of Christ could never be in doubt. Had He not commanded His followers to love their enemies? Had He not set as examples such despicable heretics as the Samaritans? Had He not accepted the company of pagan after pagan, even to the point of aiding them by miracles? Even better, had He not since His death and glorious Ascension made His will quite plain to all? Peter, Prince of the Apostles, believing Jew and strict observer of the Mosaic Law, had received during a vision a formal order from the Divine Master to baptize a pagan — a Roman centurion named Cornelius — and although more than a little surprised, had done so.[5]

For Saul, the Lord's meaning was clear. The Gospel was not to be restricted to a tiny nucleus of the Chosen People; neither was its dissemination to await the conversion of Israel. The Gospel must be proclaimed to the world, to all humanity, pagans as well as Hebrews, the poor as well as the rich. A new breed of men was about to be born who would be neither

[5] Acts 10.

11

Greeks nor Jews, neither slaves nor free men — only brothers in Christ.

After a bitter argument that was ended only by a council meeting in Jerusalem, Saul managed to communicate his burning conviction to the heads of the Church, a conviction summed up by the title that the convert of Damascus was to carry through the centuries. In the eyes of all Christendom, the first of the missionaries was to be known by the cognomen that expressed his belief in the highest universality of the revelation: Apostle to the Gentiles.

Let us look at the wandering life this frail missionary was to make his own for the twenty-two years until his death. His days were filled with unbelievable activity. Always on the move, he preached, argued, and convinced. New churches sprang up in his tracks. No sooner was one established than he traveled on to plant another seed. But he always found time to write — or rather, to dictate — those superb letters to his spiritual children, the young Christian communities. His celebrated letters touched on every matter that might prove useful to them, lavishing pertinent practical advice, and yet teaching the most sublime concepts of the new religion. What overwhelming success in twenty years, and how little failure!

What means were at his disposal for the accomplishment of so gigantic a task? There was little, apparently. He was only a humble Jew, living by the work of his own hands. His health was not good, subject to crises that he himself confessed to be painful. But he was a dauntless man whom nothing could stop when then the service of the Christ was concerned — neither prison, nor brute force, nor the threat of death. "I have been afflicted, but never crushed; stripped of everything, yet never in despair; struck down, yet never vanquished,"[6] he cried with quiet pride; and it was the simple truth. His faith was indeed that which the Christ said could move mountains. The mountains that Saul overturned were those of ignorance, laziness, violence, and misunderstanding.

The travels of the Apostles to the Gentiles are usually divided into three long missionary journeys; but these distinctions are arbitrary, for the stops between trips were very short, and there was little to differentiate one campaign from another. Saul traveled some fourteen thousand miles in the service of the Master over thirteen years.

His first mission, from the year 45 to the year 49, covered Cyprus, Asia Minor, the highlands of Pamphylia, Pisidia, Lycaonia, Derbe, Pisidian Antioch, Iconium, Lystra, and a return to Antioch. The end of the year 49 brought him back to Jerusalem for a very important meeting of the Church Council. Immediately afterward, he left for Asia Minor again to visit the Christian communities he had created and to push on to Galatia to preach to the Celtic colonies there, remnants of old Aryan rovers related to the Gauls, who centuries before had ventured into far places. Then, guided by the Spirit, he crossed the sea to Europe, where his stops were Philippi in Macedonia, Thessalonica, Athens, and Corinth, from which he crossed the sea to Ephesus in Asia Minor again. He was

[6] Cf. 2 Cor. 4:9.

back in Antioch again at the end of autumn, A.D. 52. Six months later, he was off on his third and last voyage. He retraced his steps to Ephesus to continue the work he had started there, then returned to Greece to see his friends in Corinth. He touched the shores of the Adriatic, then returned home by way of the isles that fringe the coast of Asia Minor — Mytilene, Chios, Samos, and Rhodes — and the ports of Syria and Palestine. By the time of Pentecost in A.D. 58, he was back in Jerusalem where his destiny was awaiting him.

It would be impossible here to try to follow these thirteen years of travels step by step. The complete story, both moving and picturesque, will be found in the Acts of the Apostles, written with quiet power and admirable accuracy by St. Luke, the Apostles' companion. The narrative even sparkles with comic incidents, such as the one at Lystra during the first journey. After Saul had cured a cripple there, the pagan crowd cheered him and, taking him for the god Hermes, tried to drag him to the altar to be worshiped. The good Barnabas, whom the townsfolk had decided was Zeus in person, had all the trouble in the world convincing the people of Lystra that he and Saul were not Greek gods.[7]

But the sublime far outweighs the comic in the story of Saul. One sublime incident took place in the same city of Lystra at a later date. Saul had been seriously hurt by anti-Christian mobs, and as he lay in agony, surrounded by his disciples, Christ appeared to him. Suddenly and mysteriously his many wounds became five, concentrated in the pattern of the

[7] Acts 14:8-17.

stigmata of the Passion, the gaping flesh wounds of the Crucifixion in his hands and feet and in his right side. The scars remained with him all his life.

How many episodes of these great missionary adventures might be cited here for their significance and for the moral that might be drawn from them! Take, for example, the story of Saul on the Isle of Cyprus, where the islanders worshiped Aphrodite, the goddess of love. By the power of his words, the apostle brought forth a healthy, vigorous Christian community on the pagan island — so vigorous, in fact, that Sergius Paulus, the Roman proconsul, asked to meet the herald of the new doctrine. The proconsul was an intelligent, cultivated man who was deeply interested in religious matters, like many contemporary pagans who, dissatisfied with the old formalist religion and unable to accept mythology, were groping toward the truth. So Saul met this man and spoke to him about the Christ. He convinced him of the truth of the Gospel, and the two men became such fast friends that the missionary abandoned his Jewish name of Saul and adopted that of his Roman protector: Paulus. So the name that was to be his for glorious eternity became Paul.

Paul now found himself at the far-westerly point of Asia Minor, not far from the city of Troy, where the Homeric heroes were still venerated in memory. He was ill, worn out from his long months of travel, and struggling with endless problems. Perhaps he had been thinking of taking a rest. But in his tireless missionary brain, an idea had been stirring as relentlessly as a feeling of remorse. The ancient land of Asia ended at the sea; just beyond the narrow arm of the sea lay Europe, a Europe still pagan, a Europe waiting to know Christ and His doctrine. One night, Paul was still pondering his idea when he had a vision: a man wearing the chlamys and tall headdress of Macedonia. The man was calling to Paul, begging him to carry the Light to Europe. Paul understood. There was no choice but to obey. Tired as he was, the apostle moved on once more.

New difficulties were awaiting him in Europe, quite different from any he had yet encountered. In the cities of Asia, his enemies had been either pagans whose gods he was seeking to displace, or fanatical Jews who hated him as a follower of Him who was crucified. In Athens, the intellectual center of the western world, he was up against another adversary: a mocking skepticism. The brilliant young men of Europe who had come to Athens to study were accustomed to taste all doctrines but to believe in none. Athenian youth liked to enjoy life to the dregs, and the great Christian precept of renunciation held little fascination. So when Paul appeared to speak at the public marketplace, he was met with jeers, catcalls, and quibbling taunts. His declaration that Christ had been resurrected evoked a great burst of laughter. "We shall hear thee about this yet again," someone in the crowd shouted.[8] It was all very discouraging, and Paul might easily have decided that nothing could be done with people like the Athenians.

But the apostle was not easily discouraged. The mark of a great missionary is tenacity, the stubborn refusal to admit defeat after a first setback, the infinite patience and determination to return to the attack again and again. Since Athens was

[8] Acts 17:32.

eluding him, he would push on to Corinth, the great port nearby.

Corinth was not exactly an intellectual center. It was a center of many other aspects of life, of varying degrees of honesty and decency. The most primitive precepts of morality seemed beyond the reach of most Corinthians. What matter? Had not Christ spoken gently to the woman taken in adultery and forgiven the good thief? Well, in the lower port of Corinth, among the dockers, the porters, and the waterfront toughs, Paul succeeded in sowing the good seed. A vigorous Christian community sprang up, loyal and zealous, that was always to have a favorite place in the apostle's heart and was the subject of two of his most admirable letters, the famous letters to the Corinthians.

We come now to the last stage. It was toward the end of his third voyage. Paul was heading back toward Palestine. He had, it would seem, accomplished a tremendous task, but he was not satisfied. Deep in his heart he blamed himself because vast hordes of mankind were still unaware of Christ. He had not yet finished his work. Disturbed, anxious, he retired to Miletus among his followers, who begged him to stay with them. There were rumors of an ambush awaiting him in Jerusalem. His life was in danger. But was not this the supreme testimony that he owed to the Lord: to sacrifice his life and thus complete in his own flesh the Passion of Christ? He would go to Jerusalem. And while his friends, kneeling on the beach, asked him for his supreme benediction, he embarked, knowing full well the tragic fate that awaited him, but knowing equally well that truth must have blood in order to triumph.

∞

What Paul expected came to pass. He had scarcely arrived in Jerusalem before the Jewish fanatics rose up against him.

"Behold the blasphemer!" they cried. "Behold the rebel, the profaner of the Temple!" Whenever the apostle tried to speak in his own defense, riots broke out. The situation threatened to get out of hand — until the Roman Tribune, Lysias, ordered the arrest of the missionary. An agitator? A few well-placed lashes should serve to beat a little sense into him. Paul, however, protested loudly. From his father he had inherited the title of "Roman citizen." A Roman citizen cannot legally be beaten. The Roman official reluctantly countermanded his order and decreed simply that the apostle must remain in Jerusalem. He changed his mind again when the Jews of Jerusalem appeared to be hatching another plot, and sent Paul to Caesarea, headquarters of the Imperial Roman Procurator.

Month after month, Paul languished in prison, awaiting trial on charges the Roman authorities could not decide to bring. His efforts to be released got nowhere. The delay drove him close to distraction. There was so much work still to be done, so many countries still waiting for the Word of Christ. And the man who could bring it to them was rotting away in a jail in a seaport town. Well, there was one way to force a decision. As a Roman citizen, he still had the right of appeal to the emperor. At least he would get a trip to Rome and a chance to get on with his job.

The expedient was a dangerous one, for the current Roman emperor was none other than Nero. Rome was already an uneasy place for Christians, and with a maniac on the throne, who could tell what new mad cruelties might be in the making? No matter. If his presence in Rome could serve the cause of the Christ, Paul would not hesitate. He made his appeal as a Roman citizen and asked to be sent to Rome to present his petition to the emperor.

His Roman voyage, from September A.D. 60 to the spring of 61, as told in the Acts of the Apostles, is a true adventure. He sailed on a ship of the Orient line, which followed a leisurely course to Italy via the ports of Syria and Asia Minor, Crete, and Malta. Paul took advantage of every port of call to sow with lavish hand the seeds of the Gospel. Wherever the ship stopped, a new Christian community came into being. His prestige was great — so great, in fact, that one day when a violent storm overwhelmed the small craft, and the panic-stricken crew prepared to abandon ship, Paul took command and restored order aboard. How could anyone doubt that God was with this man?

At Malta another incident seemed to prove this point. As Paul was sitting before a fire, he held out his hands to warm them at the very moment that a viper squirmed out from a bundle of twigs to escape the flames and coiled itself around the fingers of the apostle. To the accompaniment of startled gasps from his friends, Paul gently shook the viper loose and displayed his fingers to show they had not been bitten.

Italy, the Bay of Naples, Puteoli. Then up the Appian Way by easy stages toward Rome. The news of the apostle's imminent arrival had preceded him to Rome, and groups of Roman Christians went out to meet the most illustrious missionary of the Christ. The Christian community in the Eternal City was already of considerable importance. Not only were the adherents of the new religion numerous among the artisans and the little people living in the riverbank sections along the Tiber, but there were Christians in the upper classes, including even the court of the emperor. The head of this community was a wise, handsome old man who was visibly enveloped in an aura of holiness: Peter, Peter himself, the Prince of the Apostles, who had been forced to flee Jerusalem and, after a short sojourn in Antioch, had come to live in the imperial capital. His presence there was to make Rome henceforth the capital of the Christian world.

The growth of the Church of Christ could hardly escape the notice of the pagans. The Roman populace began to talk about the deeds and movements of the baptized — too much so, in fact, for absurd and odious legends were being circulated. Someone who had overheard the words of the Eucharist — "Eat, this is my Body. . . . Drink, for this is my Blood" — spread the idiotic story that these Christians were in some manner cannibals. It was also whispered that the authorities were preparing to intervene.

The Christians gave heed neither to the ridiculous gossip nor to the threats. They continued to live fraternally, helping one another, fervently celebrating their glorious rites. No sooner had Paul arrived than he joined forces with Peter to make new conversions, even though he was under constant Roman surveillance. His reputation spread so rapidly that many pagans who were sympathetic to the new doctrine came to see him. Paul also took advantage of his enforced breathing spell to write more letters, rich in precept, to the "daughter churches" he had founded.

When he was released, doubtless in the year 62, Paul left at once for Greece and Asia Minor to give his final instructions to his friends and spiritual children, for he knew that his release was no more than a respite from certain death. Deep in his heart, did he perhaps not long for martyrdom?

Arrested once more, he was sent again to Rome, where he knew what fate awaited him. "The time of my departure is at hand," he wrote to his friend Timothy. "I have fought the good fight; I have accomplished the course; I have kept the Faith. For the rest there is laid up for me the crown of justness which the Lord, the just Judge, shall award me on that day."[9] He was not mistaken.

The situation of the Christians in Rome was becoming worse. The tide of popular hate was rising against them, augmented by the winds of malice and stupidity. The slightest incident would touch off tragedy, and that incident — not at all slight — was not long in coming. On the night of July 18 of the year 64, fire broke out in several parts of Rome and spread rapidly. Fanned by the wind, it soon ate its way through entire sections of the city. By morning, the conflagration had become a spectacle of horror that lasted 150 hours. When the holocaust was finally under control, two-thirds of the capital had been reduced to smoking ruins.

Rumors began to spread through the stricken populace: the fire had been deliberately set; the emperor himself had ordered

9 2 Tim. 4:6-8.

the arson, partly for his own entertainment and partly because he had plans for rebuilding the city according to his own whims. The popular clamor increased to the point where Nero was frightened. He needed a scapegoat to divert the anger of the mob away from himself.

What about the Christians? Were they not enemies of the human race? Did not their books predict that the anger of their God would be unleashed upon the earth in a cataclysm that would destroy the world? The Christians were the guilty ones!

Then the persecutions began, savagely, atrociously. Christians were attached to stakes in public parks, anointed with pitch and resin and set afire. Others were sewed into the skins of wild beasts and thrown to vicious dogs. Hundreds were tortured in the circus at the foot of Vatican Hill before being decapitated or crucified. When the venerable apostle Peter was led to crucifixion, he insisted on being nailed to the cross head down, since he deemed himself unworthy of suffering the same torment as the Master.

As a Roman citizen, Paul was protected from torture and ignominious execution. For him the punishment was to be decapitation. He was led from the city on the road that ran toward the sea and beheaded with a stroke of the sword. Thus ended the testimony of the man who, since that August day on the sandy road to Damascus when Jesus had called him by name, had obeyed the orders of the Master to the letter, had so well sowed the earth with the seed of the Good Tidings, the first of all the missionaries, the Apostle to the Gentiles.

St. Martin

∽

Foe of Idols

Autun, a charming little city graced by an eleventh-century Gothic cathedral and a twelfth-century castle, was in the year 380 already a fine, thriving market town, the capital of the Morvan region of Burgundy. On market days, people came from leagues around to sell their cattle and their timbers. Autun's school — one might say its university — was renowned for its wise teachers and learned scientists. Fine monuments rose from the squares of Autun, its public baths, its amphitheaters, and its temples. There were many temples, all pagan, of course, for that part of what is now France was still largely heathen.

The spokesmen for Christ, however, had been hard at work in Gaul for more than three centuries, stubbornly sowing the good seed of the Gospel. The story was current that shortly after the drama of Calvary, a group of the followers of Jesus, fleeing from Palestine, had landed near Marseilles — St. Lazarus, who had been raised from the dead,[10] and his two sisters. And

[10] Cf. John 11:1-44.

23

in any event, two hundred years had already passed since St. Pothinus, St. Vitus, St. Attalus, and the gentle little St. Blandina had borne witness to the vitality of the Christian Faith by shedding their blood in the Roman arena at Lyons. Since then, the blood of these heroic martyrs had become, as one devout writer put it, "the Christian seed," sprouting churches here and there throughout Gaul. And in the third century of our era, the great missionaries who were sent out from Rome founded living communities of the faithful — St. Gaiten, St. Trophime, St. Austremoine, St. Saturnin, and St. Denis, the martyr of Paris — and left behind them a lasting memory of their vast and heroic works.

However, their work was not enough. The big cities had large nuclei of baptized souls, and the number had been growing steadily since 313, when the Emperor Constantine had authorized the practice of the Christian religion and the Emperor Theodosius had announced his intention of making the Gospel the law of his states. But the countryside lagged far behind. Throughout Gaul the peasants continued to worship some block of stone that was supposed to be a druidic monument; or a pagan altar dedicated to the sun god; or a majestic old tree that they considered sacred. Almost everywhere in Gaul, pagan immolation rites gushed red with the blood of sacrificial animals, and the festivals found the ancient divinities of Gaul more or less mixed up with the gods of Rome.

When the peasants of the Morvan came to Autun on this particular market day, they first made their usual leisurely visit to the temple to sacrifice a calf or a lamb, or, should they be plump and prosperous, a pair of white bullocks to propitiate the particular god charged with the fertility of their fields and the protection of their crops.

The market-day crowds jostled each other in the Autun streets, moving to and from the temple. Suddenly the movement stopped, and a murmur passed from mouth to mouth. A man was elbowing his way through the densely packed square, followed by a little group carrying axes, pickaxes, and mattocks. The murmur formed words: "Martin . . . Martin of Tours . . . Martin the Bishop!"

The man advanced calmly. He was clad in a cloak of rough wool such as slaves and the poorest of peasants might wear, but his bearing, his features, his expression — everything in him — bespoke quiet authority and nobility of soul. He pushed through the crowd without looking to the right or left, heading directly for the pagan temple. Before anyone realized what he was doing, the job was done. Martin attacked the columns with a pickaxe. His axe smashed the panel of a door. A section of wall crumbled. His companions, working assiduously beside him, were soon joined by Christians in the crowd.

The pagans were stupefied, too stunned even to react. Were they afraid that the demolition had been authorized by the Imperial Roman Police? Perhaps they reasoned that, since their gods had been unable to defend their own temples, their great powers had been exaggerated. Besides, the name of Martin was surrounded with tremendous prestige — a powerful man who could perform miracles, tame wild animals, heal the sick, and even resurrect the dead. A magic circle of respect and terror seemed to form around him to protect him from the fury of the mob.

While his Christian missionaries were wrecking the pagan temple, Martin crossed the square to a tall tree, a giant pine that was venerated by the peasants of the Morvan as a manifestation of some sylvan deity. He walked directly to the fine rugged trunk that rose straight to heaven. As he swung his axe, a shout arose from the crowd. This was too much! To kill a sacred tree was murder; to slash into godly flesh a crime! The cry went up: "Not the tree! Not the tree!"

The great missionary bishop was happy. This was exactly the chance he wanted, to show these people that there was nothing of a god about this tree, that it could be cut down with impunity, that the divinity whose sap they believed to be its soul would not even fight back.

"This is only a tree," Martin said, facing the crowd. "The forests are full of so-called divinities like this. The true God is the creator of all trees, but He is not Himself a tree. Let me fell this pine, and you will see that nothing will happen."

A long argument ensued. The bishop spoke. He explained the Christian doctrine. He told the pagans how vain their faith in their idols, their sacred trees, and their mystical dolmens was.

At last, someone in his audience threw down a challenge to the Christian saint. "We will not oppose your cutting down the tree," he said, "on one condition. You will remain standing under the tree when it starts to fall, on the side toward which it will fall, and you will catch it in your arms. Since you say your God is all-powerful, you will risk nothing; your God will stay the tree in its fall. But if you are crushed to death, we will know that you have been lying to us."

"I accept," Martin said simply.

He swung his axe against the trunk again and again. The notch widened. Resin oozed from the gash like pale blood from a wound. A hush settled over the crowd, broken only by the "thwack, thwack" of Martin's axe. The pagans were impressed. Much as they wanted their own gods to prove the stronger, they admired the quiet courage of the Christian.

Suddenly there was an ominous creaking. The ropes attached to the branches grew taut. A sharp crack — and the final wedge of tree trunk snapped. The fine old tree shuddered, tottered, and began to lean toward Martin. The bishop seemed not to see it. His eyes closed, his hands clasped, he prayed, and the Christians in the crowd prayed with him. Their bishop, their saint, was about to be crushed to death before their eyes. The suspense was agonizing.

Then an extraordinary thing happened. At the very instant the tottering pine began to lean and fall, Martin raised his arms in a gesture of benediction. Instantly the pine seemed to hesitate and then, as though pulled back by some invisible power, twisted around and fell in the opposite direction.

A terrified howl surged from the crowd. Tranquil, his face radiant, the saint chanted a hymn of thanksgiving. The bewildered spectators fell to their knees.

Who was this man who could risk such bold action, this witness of God to whom the All-Powerful was so visibly according His support?

He was born in the year 316, far from Autun, very far from Gaul, in fact, in that country of Central Europe then called Pannonia and which was later to be known as Hungary. His father, a "federated Goth," that is, a barbarian officer in the service of Rome, was a tribune in command of a garrison in Pavia, Italy. It was here that Martin grew up, where he first met the Christian priests under whose influence (unknown to his pagan parents) he learned to love Christ and the Gospel.

A simple "auditor" — we would call him a student of the catechism — he listened eagerly to the wise and holy men explaining to him the doctrine of love. His young heart made its decision early: He would serve the living God; he would carry His Word. He would become a monk, like the titans of prayer who lived in the deserts of Egypt and whose prowess and miracles thrilled him through and through.

Roman law, however, was at odds with Martin's wishes. At this time, the son of a soldier could pursue no other career than that of a soldier. Thus, at the age of fifteen, Martin was obliged to put on the armor and helmet of a Roman legionary. Forced into a career he did not like, he resolved to work at it as little as possible. He would become an officer. He applied for and was admitted to the School of the Clibanaries, an imperial institution in which the sons of good families studied military science and wore silver armor and helmets, plumed with great red horsetails, and long, flowing white cloaks. At the age of eighteen, he was named "Circuitor" — a rank roughly equivalent to second lieutenant — and for the first time, he commanded men.

But deep in his heart there dwelled another love, far different from that of military exploits, and secretly he remained faithful to the Word and to the vows he had taken on the altar of an Italian church.

But it was far from Pavia that he was finally to fulfill those
vows. The famous episode that the name of Martin always
evokes took place in Gaul, at Amiens, on the banks of the
Somme River. The young Roman officer had always been considered a little odd by his brothers-in-arms at the Amiens garrison. They could not understand his treating his slave-orderly
as though he were a man, even helping him carry heavy bur-
dens. Did not Martin know that a slave was not really human,
hardly more than an ox or an ass?

Martin's charity was to reach even more extravagant forms.
It was a bitter winter morning (and the winter of 338-339 was
particularly bitter in Picardy) with a numbing fog that clung
to the snow, froze on the face, and penetrated the warmest
clothing to chill a man to the bone. The young lancers officer
was returning from a tour of night inspections, wrapped to the
chin in his great cloak lined with lambskins. Despite the thick
wool, Martin was cold, for he had given his warm clothing
underneath to a group of shivering children he had encountered during a stop at some wretched village. Arriving at one
of the gates of Amiens at dawn, Martin saw a miserable creature huddled in a recess of the city wall, shivering, his teeth
chattering. Martin reined in his horse for a closer look; the
man was almost naked. The peasants were already streaming
into town with their vegetables and their rabbits to sell, but
none of them gave a second look to the miserable bundle of
rags.

Suddenly the Roman officer knew what he must do. God
must have placed this poor man in his way intentionally. He
remembered the words of Christ: "Inasmuch as you did it to

the least of these my brethren, you did it to me."[11] Yet he had nothing left to share with the less fortunate but his cloak, his fine warm cloak, which had cost him dearly. Without a second's hesitation, Martin drew his sword and slashed the thick material in two. He handed half to the derelict and spurred his horse homeward, ready to face the laughter of his barrack-mates with quiet patience.

The following night, Martin had an extraordinary dream. While he slept, Jesus rose before him, smiling tenderly, surrounded by the flutter of wings. He heard soft voices saying, "Martin! Martin, look! Do you notice nothing?" Soon the voice of Christ Himself was heard. As He unfolded the piece of fleece-lined material wrapped around the holy wounds of His body, Jesus said, "Martin, the simple catechumen, has covered me with this cloak."

This ineffable vision convinced the young Christian that he must go the whole way into the ranks of the faithful. He would be baptized. On Easter night of the year 339, at the age of twenty-two, Martin was immersed in the soul-purifying waters.

But could he remain in the service of war when at heart he belonged to the service of God? His own viewpoint and that of his superior officers differed widely. His first efforts to be released from the army were met with routine punishment. It took nothing short of a miracle to attract serious attention to his desire to devote himself entirely to Christ: He went into battle unarmed; instead of fighting, he faced the enemy, knelt,

[11] Matt. 25:40.

and prayed; the enemy surrendered. His commander, properly impressed, recommended to the emperor that Martin be transferred from the combatant services to the friars' militia.

In Pavia, he had decided to become a monk; in Gaul, he became one. Providence, so obviously watching over this exceptional soul, next faced him with the most important Christian in Gaul: St. Hilary, Bishop of Poitiers. Hilary was an admirable man of God in every way. He had commanding presence, the natural distinction of the born aristocrat, culture, eloquence, and above all the greatest of Christian virtues: humility, chastity, and charity. Martin could not have placed himself in better hands than those of Hilary.

Martin took up his solitary post at Ligugé, a little town not far from Poitiers. In imitation of the monks of Egypt, he passed months in retreat as absolute as possible, praying all day long, eating nothing but roots and herbs, the living model of renunciation for the love of God.

His example was contagious. Several souls of great faith came to follow his example. After a short trip to his native Pannonia, to which his father had retired and where he hoped to bring his parents into the Faith, he returned to Ligugé. His hut became the center of a growing community of monks. Other huts went up around him, each housing a man leading the same life of prayer, singing the glory of God, and offering to the Lord the sacrifice of all worldly joys. The ideal spread. Ligugé became a shining example, and to the people of the region, the name of Martin was synonymous with saint.

One day a little group of earnest men crossed the peaceful moors to the huts of the monastery. They were from Tours, the big city of the Loire Valley, whose bishop, St. Lidoire, had just died. The good Christians of Tours had unanimously decided that the new bishop should be the most venerated man of the valley: Martin.

Sooner said than done, however. It would be difficult to entice the good monk of Ligugé away from his cherished solitude to take up the heavy episcopal duties in Tours. So a stratagem was evolved. They would send a delegation to Martin, begging him to come to the city to heal a woman of great virtue who was dying. Out of charity, Martin agreed, and on the highway, he was ambushed by zealous devotees who made him prisoner and carried him off to Tours to become bishop. He protested in vain. They would not accept his refusal. They ignored his indignation. At last he interpreted the supplications of these good people as proof that Heaven wanted him to become bishop. And he allowed himself to be consecrated.

To be the bishop of a city like Tours was no sinecure. The Roman Empire was in decline. The Germans were already infiltrating into the rich, far-flung provinces in advance of the armed invasions to come later. Roman officials, aware of the weakness of their central government, took little interest in their duties except to milk the public funds for their personal gain. In the midst of this general disorder, a popularly elected bishop was a man of primary importance. In addition to presiding at liturgical ceremonies, preaching in the cathedral, and directing the clergy under his authority, he was continually called upon to take part in lay matters — defending the faithful against extortionist tax collectors, overseeing schools, and caring for the sick and the needy. The bishop was in fact the true chief of the city.

Martin's election as Bishop of Tours was greeted by the bishops of surrounding regions with a great chorus of laughter. The business of being a bishop required great intelligence, training, and science. Tilting a lance and throwing a javelin seemed strange apprenticeship for a complex job of administration. And how was he going to get along with the imperial authorities, this hairy monk in his fuzzy fustian robes that smelled of old rags, when the bishop had business with the provincial governor?

The laughter died down surprisingly fast, however. Not only did Martin adapt himself in no time to the difficult tasks he had assumed, but it was soon evident that he was superior in all ways to his fellow bishops in that part of Gaul. When a man is touched by the Holy Spirit, what genius can equal him?

His reputation grew rapidly. He was called upon to render the judgments of Solomon for people from all over Gaul. As his people saw him during the high ceremonies, advancing into the choir, clad only in the humble robes of the recluse and carrying as his crosier an old crooked stick, they might have wondered — until he opened his mouth. From the moment he started to speak, his audience was in his hands. For hours they would listen to him, chatting about everyday matters, the things that were closest to the hearts of his listeners, as well as about questions of Faith and high doctrine. Furthermore, his charity was evidently inexhaustible. He would always be the man who, for God's sake, had shared his cloak with a wretched beggar. Legend would have it that since that time, he had often distributed his clothing to the poor, including the vestments that should have served him at Divine Office. He was a great builder, too, eternally crossing and recrossing his diocese to erect a church wherever a Christian community was springing up.

Since Martin was obviously endowed by the Lord with great thaumaturgical powers, the halt, the lame, and the sick were always brought to him for the laying on of hands; or he was summoned to their bedsides. That he healed the sick there was no doubt. But many stories traveled by word of mouth that were more than astonishing.

For example, during one pilgrimage, a bear devoured the ass on which the saint was riding. Martin immediately ordered the bear to take the place of the ass and to act henceforth as beast of burden. That is why the toy bears of children in France are always called Martin, in memory of the saint's bear.

Another example: The saint was called to the bedside of a dying man and, after leagues of cross-country walking, arrived only to find that he had been dead for three days. Martin stretched himself out upon the corpse and breathed life into his lips, mouth to mouth. In a few moments, the man's heart began to beat again, his cheeks took on new color, and his limbs stirred.

Such prodigious performances won the new bishop a tremendous reputation. Once he was held up by common brigands on the highway, professional highwaymen who lived by what they could steal from the unfortunate traveler. When by chance they stopped the carriage of the Bishop of Tours, they fell to their knees at the first mention of his name; and when he tolerantly offered to forgive them, they promised to reform. Prominent persons, too — many of them with morals not much better than those of the highwaymen — came to sit at his feet and listen to his counsels. Martin gave them the same rebukes, read them the same lectures, and meted out the same penance.

The emperor himself heard of the prowess of the Bishop of Tours, and when he came to Gaul on an inspection tour, he summoned Martin to his capital at Treves, on the Moselle's banks. Martin came, but he minced no words in telling the emperor what he thought of him — of how he had seized the imperial throne by murder and treachery. The emperor listened without a defensive word. He dared not brave the power of God that this ex-Roman officer so obviously possessed.

Martin was not blinded by the glory that was his in his lifetime. He never lost sight of his goal, his only goal, to serve God in renunciation and penitence. The Lord had wanted him to leave Ligugé to assume the duties of a bishop, but He had not forbidden the bishop to live as a monk. So Martin had founded a monastery at Marmoutiers, a short distance from Tours, which soon attracted a swarm of saintly souls. Martin himself, after a busy episcopal day, would repair to its cloisters for evening prayers and to sleep beside his brothers. Divine Office would find him enthusiastically raising his voice with those of the choristers. It was not long before the monastery proved too small, and sister abbeys had to be created to provide outlets for so much tireless activity. When Martin died, two thousand monks came from his various monasteries to pray at his funeral — an admirable radiation from a saintly life lived in sublime simplicity.

∞

And yet his great success, fine as it was, did not completely fill the heart of St. Martin. For truly great men, the measure of importance is not what has been accomplished but what remains to be done. Often in the evening, as he stood on the terrace at Marmoutiers, surrounded by the veneration of his spiritual children, watching the sunset glow suffuse the gentle vistas of the Loire Valley, uneasiness settled over him: Had he done enough for the Christ?

Well he knew that throughout the countryside of Gaul, there were hundreds and thousands of good people who had never heard the Good Tidings, who continued to worship absurd gods, sylvan deities, mysterious forces, or even worse. In contemporary Latin, the word *paganus,* which had meant "peasant," began to mean "pagan," for it was particularly in the rural districts that superstition and idolatry persisted. Could a man of God, a spokesman for Christ, remain inactive as long as Teutatès, Belenus, and Arduina ruled over so many hearts and minds — as long as the sun, the lightning, or a big tree, a river, or a brook were objects of worship? Martin's answer was, of course, no.

Martin would go forth into the country. His assistants could competently take care of the affairs of the diocese during his absence. The monastery at Marmoutiers was a model of order and efficiency and could safely be left to itself. So Martin would go forth into the deepest backwoods of Gaul. He would speak to the crowds. He would ask them, "What are your gods?" And many would be unable even to name them. Then with his warm, vibrant eloquence that even the simplest could understand, but which even the most cultured could not help admiring, he would explain Christianity. He would tell the story of the life and death of the Lord. He would make clear to all who heard him the meaning of the sublime message sent forth to the world some three hundred years ago from the hills of Palestine.

He traveled first through the rural regions of his own diocese, then through the neighboring provinces. Maine, Anjou, and Britanny saw the little caravan of the saint and his companions, dressed in rough fustian like the peasants themselves, carrying no baggage and no change of clothes, poor and humble, as prescribed by the Scriptures for apostles bearing the word of God. The reputation that preceded them into every village drew a crowd of the curious. Martin spoke. Often he healed the sick. Always he invited his listeners to give up their false beliefs, to tear down the pagan temple that sheltered their idols, to fell the sacred tree that they believed to be the abode of some god. Sometimes he met resistance. Sometimes the saint and his crew were threatened with bodily harm. They were not intimidated.

Soon people were asking for him throughout Gaul. He appeared in Chartres, where he exorcised an unhappy child who had been made mute by the demon possessing him. He was seen in the neighborhood of Paris, the future capital of what would be France, delivering his blessings. He came back to Amiens, his old garrison town, and went to pray at the city gate, where Christ had crossed his path in the form of a half-naked beggar. He dared to push into Auvergne, in the heart of the granitic Central Plateau, which was also the hardest core of paganism in all of Gaul.

Then he traveled down the Saône Valley at the request of vineyardists whose grapes had been badly damaged by hailstorms and who sought help from the saint. He also visited what were later to become the provinces of Franche-Comté and Dauphiné on the Swiss and Italian borders, and visitors to this part of France today may still see ancient stones bearing the inscription "Martin consecrated this altar."

The power of the Lord was visibly supporting the saint in his enterprises. The felling of the great pine at Autun was one proof of this fact. There were many others, all duly listed by the good chroniclers of the time. There was, for instance, the episode of Amboise, a charming little town on the Loire. Martin and his monks had practically convinced the authorities that the pagan cult should be suppressed. However, when it came to destroying the pagan temple and the great tower that rose above it, the townspeople balked. St. Martin was disheartened. "I can do no more, Lord," he cried, "but for Thee, all things are possible." Instantly a great storm arose, a violent whirlwind that smashed the pagan tower into a thousand bits.

Another time the bishop was attacked and wounded by some malicious men driving a team of oxen, and he was in imminent danger of being trampled to death. He had only to raise his hand and pronounce a few words for some supernatural force to hold the hoofs of the oxen fast to the ground and immobilize the whole wagon train.

Even the dead could not resist such a force. The story goes that once in some far place Martin had stopped to kneel at the tomb of a saint to pray, as was his custom. He ended his prayer with the words "Man of God, bless me." And from the depths of the tomb came a voice that terrorized those who heard it saying, "It is I, servant of God, who ask you to bless me!"

The rigorous life of fighting, preaching, and traveling, day after day, league after league, would wear out any man. But Martin was privileged to keep his faculties, his vigor, and his alertness well into his eighties. One day, however, as he came home to his brothers at Marmoutiers, he announced that his end was near. They all shook their heads incredulously. With his robustness, he would live to be a hundred. But the saint repeated his declaration; no doubt he had received a secret warning from God Himself.

Martin would have wished to die in his beloved monastery, in the little cell dug into the side of a bluff, where he had spent so many hours at prayer. However, he had received bad news from the monastery of Candes. A quarrel had broken out among the monks. Holy men they might be, but they were nonetheless men. Only Martin could re-establish peace among them. So, although he felt his strength failing, he again took to the road. Just as he could tame wild beasts, so could Martin command obedience from angry and jealous men.

With order re-established, the venerable bishop was preparing to return home when his vitality began to ebb. He still had enough energy to order that he be stretched upon a pile of ashes. A servant of Him who was Crucified must not die in his bed. And as the grief-stricken monks begged him not to leave them, he murmured, "Let me look up to Heaven and not to earth. That is where my way leads now, straight before me — the way of the Lord."

The story goes that at the very instant he surrendered his soul — one Sunday at midnight — the song of angels could be heard so distinctly that there could be no possible doubt as to its origin. Many, many leagues away, Séverin, the Archbishop of Toulouse, heard the angels singing as he was leaving the Lauds. A saint-on-earth was entering Heaven.

Apostle to the Moslems

The sky was a hard blue. The Mediterranean was as calm as a lake. Not a cloud on the horizon. The ship moored to the quay at Palma, Majorca, was motionless. It was one of those days of pure beauty when the glory of God bursts forth in all the splendors of nature.

In the ship's bow, a man stood contemplating the splendor and the glory that filled his heart. Sublime words of prayer rose from his heart. There was noise and movement all around him, the usual confusion surrounding a ship preparing to sail: officers shouting orders, porters shouting at one another, the glad banter of idlers crowding the quay to watch. That night, August 14, 1314, when the land breeze freshened, the lateen sail would be hoisted to the main mast, and the ship would move into the channel at the very hour that all the church bells of the city would ring out in honor of the Very Holy Virgin and her glorious Assumption.

The man contemplating the sea as though impatient to be beyond the horizon was a majestic old man with a very white, very long beard. His beard was so long that it reached down to the hempen girdle that served him as a belt. He wore the grayish drugget of the sons of St. Francis.[12] His feet, bare in their sandals, were hardened by years of exposure to inclement weather. A monk? Not precisely. He was a Franciscan tertiary — that is to say, a layman who has nonetheless taken the vows, assumed the monastic garb, and adopted the monastic life of his clerical brothers.

The man was attracting considerable attention among the people on the quay. Parents pointed out his fine, meditative silhouette to their children. The white-bearded old man was Ramon Lull, Br. Ramon, whom people often called "the blessed," as though he were already in Heaven. They also called him "the illustrious doctor," for he was both famous and illustrious — the most famous, most illustrious man in all Majorca. Nobody knew exactly how old he was. Some said he was eighty; others swore he was past one hundred.

He had done so many things — enough for several long lives. He had written books — novels that innumerable readers had loved, light poetry and pious hymns, philosophical theses, theological treatises, and many other things as well. He was the subject of many legends. Some people said that he had made so many experiments during his long nights among his beakers and his bottles that he had finally unveiled the best-kept secret in the world: the philosopher's stone, by which alchemists could turn any base metal into gold. Others said he

---

[12] St. Francis of Assisi (1182-1226), founder of the Franciscan Order.

had discovered the drug that would conquer death. Serious folk, however, knew that he was a remarkable man despite the myths that had grown around him.

His travels, for instance, were far from mythical. Nobody knew how many journeys he had made, but he had traveled to the ends of the earth — as it was then known. He had been received by kings in the four corners of Europe, even in distant, foggy England. He had been five times to Rome and had had long interviews with the Holy Father. He had braved the hostile Turks and at the risk of his life had made his pilgrimage to Palestine, where he had knelt before the tomb of the Lord.

Even more astonishing, two, three, perhaps four times — nobody knew exactly, because Br. Ramon did not speak much about himself — he had pushed into Moslem Africa and courageously landed on the unfriendly shores of Tunisia and Algeria to carry the Good Tidings and preach the doctrine of Christ. It was toward the coast of Africa that Br. Ramon's ship was to sail that midnight, toward the blue and silver horizon that beckoned him to service in the land of Islam where, as a missionary of the Word, he wished to raise again the Cross of the Christ, which had been overturned.

Since the beginning of the fourteenth century, the Moslems — the Arabs — had been a big factor in the thinking of Europeans, particularly the Spanish. For a long time, for some six hundred years, the horsemen of Allah had been striking deep into Christian lands, overrunning most of the Iberian Peninsula, overwhelming the Africa of St. Augustine[13] and

[13] St. Augustine (354-430), Bishop of Hippo.

the martyrs, until no one who had been baptized could consider himself happy or secure. And yet from their mountain strongholds in northern Spain, the Christian kings of Castille, Leôn, Aragon, and Navarre were patiently and heroically preparing the counteroffensive that was to reconquer their land from the Infidels, foot by foot. Two centuries earlier, the Cid, epic hero of the Spaniards, had done telling damage to the power of the Moors. The brave cavaliers of Alcantara, Calatrava, and Santiago, monk-soldiers all, fought battles worthy of the medieval chronicles.

In 1236, a few months after Ramon Lull first saw the light of day, King Ferdinand III of Castille captured Cordoba, a blow to Arab power that was the beginning of the end. Thereafter, the Infidels were contained in a narrow strip of land in the southern Spanish kingdom of Granada. Elsewhere in the noble peninsula, the Cross had been raised again; the Balearic Islands were freed of the Moslem yoke.

This was not enough for a man of God such as Ramon Lull, tertiary of St. Francis. He questioned whether the reconquest of thrones, the destruction of enemy power by the sword, was being truly faithful to the commandments of the Christ. For a Christian, Ramon believed, there were other arms than steel. "Love thine enemies."[14] The Moslems, too, were entitled to the love of the Lord. There were many of them still in Spain who had yet to hear the Good Tidings of Christ; should they be abandoned? And there were thousands — hundreds of thousands — more in Africa who had never heard of Jesus,

[14] Matt. 5:44.

of His doctrine, of His life and death, or of His Resurrection. No faithful Christian could sleep as long as these souls remained in ignorance.

For this reason, Ramon Lull was setting forth on a great adventure for the fifth time. Age and fatigue were of no account. For many years, his duty had been clearly illuminated by the light of God: to be a Missionary of Christ to the Moslems, to sow with lavish hands the Gospel seed in the sterile soil of Africa.

At last the order was given to cast off. The lines holding the ship to the quay slackened and dropped. The sail filled with the soft, cool wind from the mountains. The ship dipped and rolled gently, swung slowly about, and pointed her nose toward the vast expanse of the sea and the dark horizon beyond which many souls were waiting, unknowingly, for the light of Truth. Silently, from the depths of his heart, the Franciscan brother with the long white beard, the conquering warrior of the Holy Spirit, prayed to God that his efforts would not be in vain.

∞

This impressive old man who was going forth to risk his life to obey the order of the Lord, "Go ye therefore, make disciples of all the nations," this model of faith and Christian courage had not always been such a paragon. Far from it. The noble knight and the devout mother who gave him life found little to be proud of in their son during his youthful years.

While his father, wise and learned in the Holy Scriptures, tried to interest his son in serious studies, young Ramon gave all his time and thought to pleasure. At eighteen, instead of attending the lessons of his excellent teachers, he devoted himself to the troubadours, the wandering poets who came from Provence to sing of courtly love and beautiful ladies. His anxious parents redoubled their efforts to make him see the light, in vain. They got him a position with the Infante, the son of the King of Spain. They married him to the sweet and lovely Doña Bianca, to no avail. Ramon continued to lead the dissipated life of a frivolous youth who had an eye only for lighter things.

God, however, who can read the innermost secrets of His children, knew that beneath these sorry appearances there lay an ardent soul, and that from the day that this soul should discover the love of Christ, it would serve no other. It took no less than twelve years for the transformation to be accomplished. Ramon Lull was thirty when his life changed abruptly.

No one knows exactly what caused the change. One curious story explains it thus: One evening at sundown, Ramon was following a young woman in the street. From the rear, she was extremely attractive, with a trim figure, an appealing walk, and a young, graceful bearing. He quickened his step and was murmuring sweet words of love when suddenly she turned, and the young gallant fell back in horror. Her face was an abominable festering mass, eaten away by cancer! Ramon was so shocked, the story goes, that the same night he decided to change his way of life and devote himself to God. Whether the story is truth or legend, the fact that Ramon did suddenly become a new man after a long and painful night of debate with himself is incontrovertible. He heard himself called by God, and he answered the call.

Henceforth, his life was different. No more did he compose
light verses, which he was accustomed to sing in his warm
voice to some pretty girl. Henceforth, the only poems he would
write were to the glory of God, proclamations of his own re-
pentance: "Am I worthy to praise Thee, I who have sinned so
greatly? I am but a troubadour, and yet I love Thee." His conversion was to last more than fifty years. As in the case of St.
Paul on the road to Damascus, the sole confrontation by the
Divine Presence was enough to absorb his entire life. There
was only one question: Which of the many ways of serving
God was he to choose?

Even in the wildest moments of his mad youth, Ramon had
always shown one virtue, that of charity. He had always been
good to others, generous with his worldly goods, and ready to
be of service. Once he had resolved upon fidelity to the commandments of Christ, it was this quality of his that determined
his choice of paths. "Has not the Lord asked us to extend a
hand to the most miserable of our brothers?" he reasoned. The
many Moslems still living in Majorca and the other Balearic
Islands since the recapture of the islands by the Christians
were ruined, despised, and unhappy. It was to them that Ramon
Lull would devote himself in an effort to bring them into the
fold. Whenever he passed through the fortified city gate into
the Arab quarter, it seemed to him that the statue of the Holy
Virgin standing there was ordering him to consecrate himself
to evangelizing the Saracens.

Before making his final decision, however, he would meditate, pray, and seek counsel. He first went to see the bishop,
who talked about the Little St. of the Poor, the gentle, pious

Francis of Assisi, who had given up all his worldly possessions to devote himself entirely to God. Ramon thereupon took leave of his wife, donned the habit of a hermit, and set out on the road like a pilgrim. "The roads are long that lead to God," he sang in a poem, "but they glow with shining love."

Successively he was seen at Santiago-de-Compostela, the celebrated Spanish sanctuary, surrounded by pilgrims from all over Europe; at Montserrat, the Benedictine monastery perched high in the mountains of Catalonia; and in France at numerous shrines, notably Rocamadour on the limestone plateau of the southwest. As he trudged along the never-ending road through sun or snow, he raised his voice to Heaven in delightful songs exalting the beauty of God's world and praising the Creator. Sometimes his bare feet left bloody tracks in the snow; often he had neither food nor shelter. He made light of his troubles, offering them to Christ in expiation of his youthful sins and as a pledge of his new love.

When he returned to Majorca two years later, he was no longer the same man. The elegant, handsome youth had become thin and nervous; a beard hid his sunken cheeks. But his mind was now made up. He had taken counsel with wise and enlightened men in many places. Raymondo de Penaforte,[15] the grand old man of Barcelona who was nearly a hundred years old, had listened to him and advised him. He was certain now that God had called him to a great task. He took steps that must have been most painful to him. He renounced all his

[15] St. Raymondo de Penaforte (1175-1275), Master General of the Dominicans.

property in favor of his family. He had a guardian appointed for his children, as if he were dead. Thus, free of all worldly ties, as poor as a son of St. Francis, in whose footsteps he wished to follow, he was now ready to give himself completely to the work awaiting him: to spread the Word of God.

And the Lord rewarded him. One day, he was praying on a hilltop from which he could see only the sky and the sea, when he suddenly felt the light of the All-Powerful shining around him. He must have had a similar impression as that which was vouchsafed Moses in the presence of the burning bush. His mind became extraordinarily lucid. It seemed to him that the Virgin Mary herself had come to counsel him. In a flash of light, he could see the whole wide world with its uncounted hordes still awaiting the revelation of Christ. No, writing books and pious poems was not enough. Prayers and pilgrimages were not enough. "Go ye, therefore, and make disciples of all the nations!" The order of the Master rang in his ears. And since close at hand his Moslem brothers lived in suffering and in ignorance, he would be the Apostle to the Moslems.

∞

The first step in the evangelization of the Moslems would be to learn their language. Ramon Lull knew no Arabic, and his first efforts to learn it gave rise to a discouraging incident. He had bought a young Saracen slave, whom he treated with kindness in return for the boy's teaching him the language. The moment Ramon began to talk of Jesus Christ, however, the Moslem gave tongue to shocking blasphemous remarks. Indignant, Ramon slapped him. The young Arab said nothing at the time, but he plotted revenge, and one day when his Christian master trustingly turned his back, he stabbed him.

Saved by a miracle, Ramon thought only to secure a pardon for the slave, who had been arrested and was awaiting execution. But the day Ramon was well enough to visit the lad in prison, he was informed that the Arab had just hanged himself. This incident did much to hurry the future missionary toward his goal. He blamed himself for losing his temper with an infidel who was guilty of nothing more than being ignorant of Christ. Ramon reproached himself for not having loved the lad sufficiently.

Passionately he pursued his study of Arabic, at the same time writing books — heavy erudite tomes, which, added to the knowledge of his adventure on the hilltop, which was gradually spreading throughout his island, won him the nickname "the illustrious doctor." He was still living like a monk, still wearing the rough drugget of a Franciscan. He prayed day and night, especially to the Holy Virgin, to whom he dedicated poems full of charm and feeling.

As his former employer, the Infante, had become King Jaime II, Ramon laid his plans before him and persuaded the king to found a monastery where a little group of Franciscans could, by prayer and meditation, prepare to preach the Gospel to the Moslems. The result: Miramar, which might well be called the first of the mission seminaries. From Miramar, monks went forth to every corner of Spain and the Balearics, into the Saracen villages and the Arab quarters of the cities, to explain Christian truth to the Moslems and convert them to the Faith.

Even this was not enough. The few thousand Moors remaining in Christian Spain were not the only ones in need of the Gospel. The Arab Empire was still of vast extent, stretching from the Atlantic coast of Africa to Egypt in the east, northward to Syria and Asia Minor, and even, it was said, to the far-flung Indies. It represented an immense domain in which only the Koran was law and only Mohammed was venerated. It was here, to the very heart of the Islamic world, that the Good Tidings must be borne. And the time was now.

Miramar was founded in 1276, a period when the great Christian adventure of the Crusades seemed to have bogged down in failure. Gone were the glorious days when Godefroy de Bouillon had led his valiant and exhausted Crusaders into recaptured Jerusalem. Since that July 14, 1099, the Christian kingdoms of the Holy Land had crumbled under the combined misfortunes of misrule and Moslem attack. Less than a century before Miramar, Sultan Saladin had taken back Jerusalem, and Christian arms had never been able to retrieve the Holy City. Even the heroic and saintly King of France, Louis IX, had been unsuccessful. His first attempt ended when he was captured by the Saracens soon after landing in Egypt; his second when he died of the plague in Tunisia.

Was not this long succession of failures a sign of God's will? Since even St. Louis, a true man of God, had been unable to prevail by force of arms, was this not proof that the Moslems must be brought to Christ by other means? Had not two saints of the past century constantly proclaimed that a Crusade of Peace was worth a dozen military expeditions, that the best weapon to conquer hearts was not the sword but the mission?

Ramon Lull agreed.

Ramon believed he should seek approval of his plans at the highest level, and he took the road to Rome to open his heart to the Pope. The time seemed propitious. Not long before, the Holy Father had sent a mission, headed by Jean de Plano Carpini, a Franciscan monk, into the heart of Asia to convert the Tartars and the Mongols. The Franciscan mission had in effect crossed most of the vast continent, at great risk and with unbelievable adventures, but with little success. So while the Pope listened benevolently to Ramon, the papal advisors were less than lukewarm. Ramon's plea for schools for Arabic and other Oriental languages, for more monks to swell his nucleus of future missionaries at Miramar, fell on deaf ears in Rome. When he moved on to other Christian centers, such as Paris, he still could arouse little interest in his project.

But Ramon did not give up. His plans, he was convinced, were inspired by Christ Himself in the moment of great light on the hilltop in Majorca. Since he could get no help from men, his only recourse was to God. He left for the Holy Land.

Palestine at that time was in a sorry state, plundered by the Moslems, ruined by years of warfare. Ramon managed to reach Jerusalem, where he knelt before the empty Holy Sepulcher. As he prayed, he knew that he had not been mistaken; he was on the right road. During the long hours spent in prayer on the very spot where Jesus died so that men — all men — might receive the message of love, Ramon Lull heard a mysterious voice speaking within him, repeating the injunction that he must embark on the great adventure. And he resolved again to do so.

∞

Back at Miramar, he called together his community of monks, men who shared his Faith and hopes, who looked upon him as their guide, a guide sent by God Himself. He spoke to them calmly but fervently. The monastery no longer needed him. The work was going along well, the senior monks had the situation in hand, and neophytes were beginning to knock at the door. The founder's task had been accomplished. Therefore he would go away. He would go alone. He would sail for Africa, where he would undertake the great work that had been deep in his heart for many years. He would be missionary to the Moslems on their own soil.

He now had a perfect command of Arabic. He had made a thorough study of the doctrines of Islam so that he could argue with the most learned doctors of Koranic law. He had even written a book in the Arabic language, and during his sojourn in Palestine, he had several times engaged Moslems in discussions of their own religious problems. He returned to Rome for papal permission for his adventure, and then sailed from Genoa for Tunisia.

Ramon had no trouble landing, for in Tunisia, as in Egypt and other countries of North Africa, there were in all the big ports large colonies of Christian merchants. The Christians maintained cordial relations with the Arab authorities, since both groups profited by mutual trade. However, the Christians lived apart from the Moslems, kept to themselves, and kept their intergroup relationship on a strictly business basis. They carefully avoided the subject of religion for fear of causing bad feeling and being run out of the country. Their attitude was the exact opposite to what Ramon Lull had in mind.

Ramon dressed like a sage of Islam. With his sun-bronzed skin and his gaunt build, he could easily pass for an Arab, mingle with street-corner crowds, and take part in the religious arguments that often arose spontaneously in the marketplace from idlers gathered around some passing *imam* or Moslem savant.

For many weeks, he worked in this manner, speaking whenever he had the chance. He even argued with Mohammedan sages in their own schools while their students listened. He made such rapid progress that he was bound to overreach himself. And one day he did. He scored such an obvious verbal triumph over his adversary that the vindictive Moslem plotted vengeance. Any man who attacks the dogmas of Islam and who speaks so warmly of Jesus, of His life and His message, must certainly be a Christian — a *Roumi,* as they say in Africa. The vanquished debater ran to the authorities to denounce the *Roumi.*

Ramon Lull was arrested, tried, and condemned to death as a blasphemer of Allah and an enemy of the religion of Mohammed, his prophet. Had the hour come for the Franciscan tertiary to give the Lord bloody proof of his fidelity? Ramon was ready; he would welcome martyrdom.

But the Lord apparently still had need of him. A high-placed and influential citizen of Tunis, who had heard Ramon debating with the Moslem sages, intervened on his behalf. Whether or not the Tunisian had been swayed by the Christian arguments, he did save the missionary's life. However,

Ramon did not escape a vicious flogging, after which he was flung, bruised, bleeding, and gasping for breath, aboard a Genoese ship sailing the next morning. So Mohammed had been avenged and the Christian run out of the country. Or so the Arabs thought.

The Arabs had underestimated the courage and determination of the man of God. He had submitted patiently, even joyously, to the lash, thinking of the punishment endured by the Divine Master. But he had barely started his work. He had risked his life once. If God had not wished him to continue his task of evangelization, would He not have restrained him? After dark, Ramon jumped overboard and swam ashore.

He was too exhausted to resume his work immediately, however. He made his way back to Majorca to gather his strength and to meditate. He wondered whether it would be better to go back to writing books, after all, instead of courting danger in Africa. One day, while he was walking in the fields, deep in meditation, he came upon a hermit. He opened his heart to the hermit, telling him he could never rest as long as the Holy Sepulcher was not in Christian hands and as long as the Moslems did not recognize the Lord Jesus. The hermit replied that Ramon had indeed found the true path and his true duty, and that he should be deterred by neither obstacles nor apparent failure; that God asked only that he give his testimony with all his heart; that the rest would be granted him as surplus.

So Ramon embarked once more. He sailed alone. Nobody was eager to share his perils. They said he was mad to beard the Moor in his own den; that the Last Judgment would determine who had been mad and who had been wise. King Jaime II himself tried to deter him. The king pointed out there was plenty of work to be done in Spain and the Balearics and that Ramon would have royal permission to preach in the synagogues of the Jews and the mosques of the Moors. But Ramon was adamant. He alone knew what God had ordered him to do during the moment of great light.

This time Ramon went to Algeria. This time he disembarked boldly at Bougie. He took no precautions, made no effort at dissimulation. He appeared in the marketplace and in public squares, knowing that as soon as he started to speak, a crowd would gather, according to African custom. Once he had an audience, he immediately began his attack on the doctrine of Mohammed.

He was soon arrested and thrown into a miserable cell. The Christian merchants from Genoa and Catalonia used their influence to secure better treatment for him, and he took advantage of the bigger, lighter cell to write a long treatise in Arabic, again attacking the Islamic religion. After spending six months in prison, he was expelled from Africa once more. And the day before his ship was due to arrive in Italy, it ran into a violent storm and foundered. Ramon escaped with his life, but all his belongings were lost, including his precious Arabic manuscript. He wondered whether Providence had turned against him.

But nothing could discourage him. He stayed in Italy until he had rewritten his entire manuscript. He moved on to France to see the Pope, who was then installed at Avignon, and discuss his future plans. He attended the Council of

Vienna to agitate in favor of setting up chairs of Arabic and other Oriental languages in Christian universities. Would they understand how important it was to have men without ties and without regard for their own lives who would go forth to shout the message of the Gospel in the very face of the infidel? Many centuries later, another one of God's madmen would understand and would go forth; he, too, alone, to carry the same testimony to Moslem lands: Charles de Foucauld, who would give up his life in the Sahara.

Twice more Ramon invaded the heart of Islam. On his last journey, he was an old man, as we saw him standing in the bow of the ship about to sail from the port of Palma. He was still a fine-looking man, erect and of noble bearing, but Ramon knew that his resilience was gone. He had made his last will and testament, directing that his books be translated into the principal languages of the Occident. The Catalonian craft that was taking him to Africa for the last time was carrying a full cargo of merchandise — and the hopes of the Franciscan that at last he would succeed in bringing the Good News to the Moslem. King Jaime II had finally understood the importance of the missions and had given Ramon a letter to the King of Tunisia requesting a suitable welcome. Thanks to the Spanish king's backing, Ramon was able to speak for a whole year without interference from the Arab authorities. He was even able to send for some of his old pupils to come and help him.

The old campaigner saw himself slipping into impotence. He knew that his infirmities had already won the day, yet stubbornly and heroically he continued to fight, to preach, to write, and to publish more and more tracts and treatises arguing with the Moslem doctrine and proclaiming Christ. He knew that death was close behind him, yet he refused to look back over his shoulder.

Finally, one June day of 1316, a mob aroused against him by his Islamic adversaries rushed him off his feet, beat him viciously, and left him lying in the street, believing him dead. And he would have died, had not a group of Genoese sailors found him and carried him aboard their ship.

The ship was already at sea when he regained consciousness. He was grateful to the sailors who had brought him aboard, yet he truly regretted that he was not to die on his beloved soil of Africa, a martyr to his Faith. Despite the tender care lavished upon him by all the crew, he grew steadily more feeble. He died just as the headlands of his native Majorca rose above the horizon.

Ramon Lull was laid to rest in the soil of his own island, a heroic witness to the passion that burns in the heart of every missionary, harbinger of those who long afterward were to bring back to Africa the Cross and the love of Christ.

Father to the Indians

To recall the horrible is never pleasant, yet in this case it belongs to history. And Bartolomé de las Casas, man of God, could never have assumed the admirable role that was his, had not blood been spilled, tears shed, and almost incredible cruelty committed.

All this took place in the huge empire that the conquistadors had just presented to Spain — land that today bears the separate names of Mexico, Chile, Peru, Colombia, Ecuador, and the Dominican Republic. Torture and massacres were the law of the land. One governor, when chided by a priest for tossing live children to his dogs at mealtime, had the next child cut up before the priest's eyes. Another governor had five thousand Indian prisoners executed so that he could watch them die. Elsewhere native chiefs and minor kings, *"caciques,"* were tortured for hours until they agreed to pay ransoms of great quantities of gold and, when they had paid, were wrapped in straw and tossed on a pyre to be burned alive. And the perpetrators of these abominations claimed to be Christians.

Heroes of God

Some thirty or forty years earlier, a taciturn Genoese named Christopher Columbus had urged his three tiny caravels into the west and in 1492 sighted the unknown lands that an Italian cartographer was to name America in honor of another navigator, Amerigo Vespucci. After the explorers and the pioneers came the conquerors, men seeking gold, men who would seize the newfound lands in the interest of their personal fortunes, men of great daring and violent passions, men for whom a life — their own or another's — meant nothing. What Hernando Cortez was doing in Mexico, what Almagro and Pizarro were doing in Chile and Peru, other ambitious adventurers dreamed of doing in many other corners of the continent: conquering empires, capturing and pillaging cities, sifting gold through the fingers of their greedy hands, and becoming richer than a Spanish grandee and more powerful than a king overnight.

There was no doubt about the courage of these men. Alone, far from their own country, in a land and climate equally hostile, practically abandoned by their government, which gave them little backing, they accomplished almost incredible exploits in the face of daily danger, disease, and hardship. There is no doubt that they wrote a new page in the book of human adventure. But their risks and their suffering made them brutal, hard on themselves and others, rarely able to admit the slightest hint of charity or fraternity into their relations with the conquered peoples.

The conquered peoples were, of course, the natives who lived in the Americas long before the arrival of the conquistadors. They were called Indians, as everyone knows, because the discoverers of America thought they had reached the Indies. Far from being savages, these Indians were in many places people of a very high degree of civilization. In what is now Mexico, the land of the Aztecs, the Spaniards found big cities and impressive monuments. In what is today Peru, the land of the Incas, they were surprised to find a well-organized road system. In many of the states, they found a well-regulated social and political order that was the forerunner of what we call today "socialism." The pre-Columbian art that the Spaniards found had already achieved masterpiece proportions.

The Indians were behind the Europeans in several respects, however. They did not use draft animals. They had no firearms. They were astounded by the horses of the Spaniards, which seemed to them fantastic beasts straight from the infernal regions. Generally peaceful people, overawed by the guns and cavalry of these strangers who had invaded their land, they offered little resistance — a fact that did not guarantee them against the ferocity of their conquerors.

The great misfortune of these poor folk was that they had gold, much gold. When returning Spanish sailors told their friends that in the new world the precious metal was so plentiful that it was used to cover temples and palaces, and that the trees in the terraced gardens gleamed with golden fruits and precious stones, and that the kings had great halls loaded with priceless ingots, they caused many hearts to beat with envy and many eyes to shine with greed.

The conquistadors would stop at nothing to separate an Indian from his gold. A fever, a delirium, drove the Spaniards to make slaves of the natives. Forced to tramp miles and miles for months on end, carrying killing loads in tropical heat and torrential rains, conscripted to work in the mines while their women cultivated the fields, the Indians died like flies. What matter? One word summoned others to take the places of the missing.

Add to these destructive operations the senseless massacres, the tortures inflicted in the bloody dementia that had possessed the Spaniards, and it is easy to understand the shocking reduction in population suffered by the Indian peoples during the first half century after the discovery of their land by Europeans. The population of Cuba dropped from fifty thousand to fourteen thousand in twenty years, Santo Domingo from one hundred thousand to fifteen thousand, and in some parts of Mexico the indigenous populations were almost wiped out. It is difficult to imagine men — Europeans, and Christians, too — perpetrating such heinous crimes.

The most grievous aspect of this tragedy was that these conquerors claimed to be bringing to the Indians the law of Christ! When the Pope recognized the claims of the King of Spain to the new lands, had he not formally declared that they were to be evangelized? And did not Queen Isabella, who was a devout Catholic, frequently remind her distant lieutenants of this obligation? But the conquistadors lost no sleep over converting the Indians or giving them a spiritual life. The Indians were not worth the trouble. They were pagans, and even worse, savages who still offered human sacrifices on the altars of their gods. Even those who had been baptized by the priests accompanying the troops were still miserable slaves fit only for the most onerous tasks.

The shame of this situation stained the glorious adventure of the discovery of the New World with blood and mud. And it seemed destined to continue without remedy.

∞

In 1509, a Dominican father named Montesinos mounted to the pulpit of a church in Santo Domingo. A few months earlier, the Spanish authorities had imported a force of forty thousand conscript laborers to replace those natives who had perished in the frightful depopulation.

Fr. Montesinos had the exemplary courage to denounce the cruelty of the conquerors, even though his church was filled with soldiers who considered rape and rapine no more than the normal fulfillment of a conqueror's dream. When the Dominican priest began to enumerate the many crimes of his countrymen, his listeners forgot they were in a holy place and shouted insults and threats to the good father. Yet he continued undeterred.

He was not the first priest in the New World who had shown himself worthy of the Gospel he was sent to preach. The good Fr. Urdaneta had carried the Cross alongside the soldiers in Mexico and the Philippines and had assumed the role of advocate for the vanquished. Other monks in Mexico and in Peru had tried to start schools for Indian children. In Santo Domingo, the monastery founded by Pedro de Cordoba, to which Fr. Montesinos was attached, was widely known for its good works. Many priests had gone to the military governor to protest against atrocities. Their public denunciation of errors committed by the Spaniards was of extreme importance.

How many of their parishioners as a result took stock of themselves and wondered whether they were really behaving as Christians?

One young man did wonder — and found the answer painful. He was Bartolomé de las Casas, the descendant of a French soldier who left his native Limousin to fight the Moslems during the reign of Ferdinand the Catholic and was elevated to the nobility by the Spanish king. The spirit of adventure was passed on from father to son. The second generation of the now Spanish Las Casas sailed with Columbus on his first voyage, and the third generation, Bartolomé, who graduated from the University of Seville at twenty-four, signed on with Columbus on the great navigator's third voyage in 1498. In the years following, he sailed the seas and trod alien soil with the enthusiasm of youth and the temerity of a conquistador. And like the other conquerors, he had no thought except the capture of new lands and the acquisition of a personal fortune by any means. He had never bothered to question whether the Lord might approve the slaughter of Indians by the thousands, the seizure of their lands and possessions, or their being forced into the most abject and grievous slavery.

The sermon of Fr. Montesinos changed Bartolomé's whole life. He felt as though he had suddenly regained his sight after years of blindness. Was he not at least an accomplice in the crimes the Dominican was denouncing? His heart swelled with remorse. The shame was too much for a soul as fundamentally kindly as his. He would make amends. He would dedicate all his strength to the defense of the unfortunate Indians.

First, Bartolomé set his own slaves free. Then he went to see the good fathers who had dinned the judgment of truth into his ears, and he sought instruction. The young man's faith and good intentions were so obvious, and the New World was so much in need of clerics, that he was accepted immediately and hurried through his training.

Less than two years after he had first heard the Word of God through the voice of Fr. Montesinos, Bartolomé de las Casas was ordained. His first Mass was celebrated with great pomp, for it was in effect a triumph. Here was the son of one of the first conquistadors, a young officer on the threshold of a promising career and great riches, who was giving up position and fortune to devote himself to the work of charity and evangelization.

Once a priest, Bartolomé threw himself wholeheartedly into the thick of the fight he was to wage for the rest of his life. It was clear from the outset that he was in for a fight. The slave-owners whom the priests accused of plundering and depopulating the New World, the cruel administrators who heard themselves denounced from the pulpit for dishonoring the fair name of Spain — all ganged up on the spokesmen of Christ. They were joined by the big landowners who conscripted thousands of slave-laborers to work their plantations, and the mine-owners who also benefitted by forced labor. The priests must not be allowed to ruin the commerce and industry of the conquered countries with their fine words. Furthermore, there was the danger that the Indians might take the priests' words literally and revolt against the Spaniards. The opposition to the priests often took the form of threats and violence, but the desire to help the unhappy Indians was too deep-seated to be easily thwarted. The battle was on.

Bartolomé worked without a day of rest. He traveled over hill and dale to protect his friends the Indians. He would turn up in Cuba as parish priest for a difficult region where the Indians had been so mistreated that the very sight of a Spaniard, even one wearing a cassock, filled them with loathing. He accompanied one of the expeditions of Pánfilo de Narváez, one of the most barbarous of the conquistadors, to try to induce him to temper his treatment of the Indians. He was a Dominican monk in Nicaragua, sent by his prior to aid the bishop in converting the Indians. He appeared in the hostile mountainous land that is today Guatemala, where, accompanied by several brothers, he went unarmed among natives reputed to be warlike and bloodthirsty, and succeeded in winning them to Christ. Today in Peru, tomorrow in Mexico, next week in Santo Domingo — wherever the Word of the Lord needed to be heard or charity instilled, Bartolomé was to be found. There was scarcely a corner of the lands that have become Latin America that did not see his noble profile, his white robe, and the long black cloak of the sons of St. Dominic.[16]

He soon had a tremendous reputation among the natives, who were astonished to see a Spaniard boldly and energetically acting on their behalf. "Father to the Indians" became his nickname. So great was the veneration in which he was held that a letter from Fr. Bartolomé was enough to ensure

---

[16] St. Dominic (c. 1170-1221), founder of the Dominican Order.

peaceful reception from the most warlike of tribes. Even the terrible Narváez could expect a friendly welcome if he was accompanied by Fr. Bartolomé. Even the soldiers and landowners who hated Bartolomé recognized his saintliness. Whole villages embraced Christianity at the sound of his voice. Wherever he passed, parishes sprang up, and he was hard put to find priests to minister to these new scions of the Faith.

Once more in the history of the Church, the flame burning in the heart of its missionaries, the flame of the apostolate in the service of Christ, gave light to whole regions of the earth. Not a day passed without the ideal inspired in the young officer by Fr. Montesinos being translated into action.

Bartolomé's mission was not accomplished without difficulties, it must be admitted. There were, of course, the natural obstacles of the terrain: few roads, impenetrable jungle, wild animals, poisonous snakes, vicious stinging insects, loathsome tropical diseases — dangers common to all missionaries, whether in South America, Asia, or Africa. The natives, too, gave him trouble occasionally. Sometimes, despite the efforts of the good priest, a whole village would revolt against the cruelty and extortion of the conquerors and kill a few Spaniards, thus provoking retaliation. The Spanish punitive expedition would burn the village, put the last man to the sword, and carry off the women and children into slavery. Bartolomé, heartbroken, could only watch helplessly.

But the worst, the true obstacles came from the Spaniards themselves, from the governors, the slave-owners, the exploiters of the mineral wealth — the men who had always opposed the action of the priests. Bartolomé knew them well, for he had been one of the conquerors himself and had many old friends among them. He knew their tricks. He knew how little disposed they were to obey the king's order to treat the natives favorably and that they would go to any lengths to nullify it.

He was forced to witness many painful events. One day, a force of free laborers who had been imported into Santo Domingo were refused permission to return to their home islands and were reduced to slavery. The whole Indian population of Santo Domingo rose in angry protest and in their fury killed two Spanish Dominican missionaries. The retaliation was quick and savage. The Spanish authorities massacred not only the villages in which the priests had been killed, but destroyed every settlement in the province.

Bartolomé hurried to berate the officials who had ordered the massacre. As dreadful as was the murder of the two priests, it did not justify the wiping out of the innocent population of an entire province.

Bartolomé had scarcely begun his tirade when the counter-attack began. The governor insulted him and threatened him with arrest for subverting the Spanish authorities. Hieronymite priests accused him of complicity with the assassins. When a mob formed, Spanish officers misdirected its fury against Bartolomé. Forced to flee for his life, the missionary took refuge in a monastery.

It was not only in the New World that the Father to the Indians found trouble. As was his duty, he sent both religious and royal authorities in Spain reports on the atrocities he had witnessed. The reports were referred to the Council of the Indies, responsible for New World affairs, which duly dispatched instructions reminding colonial governors, administrators, and military officers of their Christian duties. But America was a long way from Spain, and the cruel conquistadors were deaf to words from Madrid.

Badly frustrated, Bartolomé decided that the only way to get action was to sail for Spain, go directly to the royal palace, and speak plainly to the king. He was not altogether correct, but he was persistent. He did complain to King Ferdinand, but nothing happened. When Charles V succeeded Ferdinand in 1516, he went back again with the same story. All in all, Bartolomé crossed the Atlantic five times in the interest of his Indians. It was a good idea, but its execution was impractical.

The conquistadors had too many friends and relatives in high places. The Governor of Such-and-Such Colony had a brother who was a cabinet minister. General This-or-That had a cousin who was a bishop at home. What was worse, too many important personalities of the court and government — even of the Church hierarchy — had invested money in New World enterprises, especially in mining, and were collecting fat dividends. It is not difficult to imagine with what enthusiasm these well-fixed Spaniards viewed the arrival of this fanatical missionary who sought the king's ear with his plea to abolish slavery and to regulate working conditions in the mines of the New World. They could not, of course, show open hostility to Bartolomé, for this would mark them as bad Christians. They could and did, however, work assiduously at driving a

wedge between the sovereign and the missionary, to discredit
Bartolomé as a madman. They even went to the lengths of
bringing another priest back from the Americas, a rival missionary with a grudge against Bartolomé, who convinced court
and ecclesiastical circles that the work of the Father to the Indians was dangerous to the national security of Spain and contrary to the interests of evangelization.

A man who had braved the perils of the jungle and the
most savage tribes, however, was not put off by petty intrigues.
He got to see the king several times, despite all efforts to the
contrary, and painted a vivid picture of the plight of the unhappy Indians in the face of intolerable Spanish iniquity. His
eloquence moved the king to promise new laws protecting the
Indians, but nothing he or the king could do would guarantee
that the laws would be obeyed by ruthless conquistadors or
greedy colonial governors. All his life, Bartolomé would have
to fight against the ability of wicked men to frustrate the good-
will of their rulers. But he would never stop fighting, never
stop sounding the alarm, never stop protesting against the
underhanded methods of his despicable enemies.

It was to enlighten the king, as well as the Pope, that
Bartolomé de las Casas wrote a book that summed up the
enormous documentation he accumulated on the havoc created by the conquerors: *The Destruction of the Indies*. He com-
plemented it with a diatribe against slavery and a work on the
best ways to spread the Gospel among the Indians of the
Americas. The publication caused a sensation. Bartolomé's
enemies countered with a miserable pamphlet that attempted
to refute his arguments — in vain! Christian opinion was

aroused by such grave accusations made by the pen of a man of God. How could anyone remain indifferent to the news that in the Americas men were burned alive "for the honor and reverence of our Redeemer"?

Charles V read Bartolomé's books and, devout Christian that he was, was aghast. In 1542, he called the missionary before the Grand Council of the Indies to repeat his accusations in person. He listened to the Indians Bartolomé had brought with him as witnesses, "simple, without guile, humble, patient, and faithful." He also heard the testimony of some conquistadors, "ferocious as wolves, tigers, and hungry lions." What answer could be made to such a voluminous and precise bill of particulars?

Enlightened by the reports of other priests, the Pope had just promulgated a bull condemning the terrorist methods of the conquerors. The king-emperor, too, decided on new action. New laws, stricter and more precise than the old ones, were decreed, and men of trust were sent to the New World to enforce them. The king gave the new administrators their instructions in person. The humanitarianism of Bartolomé de las Casas seemed to have triumphed at last.

Bartolomé was then seventy years old, but he had only one desire: to return to the New World and resume the great missionary work to which he had dedicated his life. When he was told that in token of his admiration, the king had nominated him for bishop, he first asked to which diocese. Learning it was to be Cuzco, in Peru, one of the richest and most important in the Americas, he demurred. It was too rich, too important. If the king really wished to confer on him the dignity of a miter, let the diocese be a very poor and difficult one, even if it had to be created to his order; and let it be in a region where the task of conversion was not yet very far advanced, so that there would still be plenty of work to be done for the Lord.

So Bartolomé was made Bishop of Chiapas in the mountains of southern Mexico, near the border of what is now Guatemala. Parts of the region were already being exploited for growing cacao, palm oils, and corn, and for raising cattle, but others were covered with jungle so dense, so infested with snakes and insects, that the Indians themselves dared not venture into it.

But Bartolomé was not to remain long in his diocese. He soon learned that the "new laws" of Charles V were not being observed much more closely than the old ones; that atrocities were still being committed; that, although slavery had been abolished in theory, it was still being practiced. So he took to the road again, plodding through the New World to defend his dear Indians. It was in this period that he thought of a way to handle the conquistadors, a method that he outlined in a new book. He ordered all priests who heard the confessions of Spaniards in the New World to question their penitents on their behavior with the Indians and on the source of their wealth, and to refuse them absolution if they did not return stolen property or if they had not freed their slaves. The majority of the clergy welcomed Bartolomé's stand and applied his ruling with great courage and firmness. The Spanish colonials, of course, were fuming with rage.

"Let our confessors be warned," declared the saintly bishop, "that in giving absolution to those who butcher the Indians and steal their gold, they become accomplices before God and will be held to account for these crimes that they may too lightly absolve."

The conquistadors put up a desperate defense against this terrible blow. Once more they sent false reports to Spain by witnesses who denounced Bartolomé de las Casas as a traitor to Spain and to Christianity. Return their property to Indians? Abolish forced labor? The whole colonial structure would crumble. This mad bishop would next be demanding suppression of porterage and abolition of the pearl fisheries.

Everyone who had ever shared in the conquistadors' booty, as well as the merchants who were supplying them, was affected by the new regulations for Confession. Riots broke out in some regions; priests who had refused absolution to notorious thieves and sadistic brutes were threatened, and then attacked. And the cause of all this trouble was, of course, this Fr. Bartolomé, this dangerous gossip, this fanatic. The king simply must call him home to explain.

The king did summon the missionary, who once more crossed the ocean. He was expected to come crawling home, apologetic and defensive. On the contrary, Bartolomé did not seek to be excused. He accused! He wrote a detailed memoir, justifying his actions, and had it approved by the highest religious authorities of the day. He recalled that it was the Pope who had entrusted the New World to the King of Spain for the purpose of spreading the Gospel to its inhabitants. The only principles that should govern Christians going to the New World, therefore, were those of Jesus Christ. The Church had the right through her confessors, therefore, to ensure the observation of those principles and to punish anyone refusing to comply.

St. Augustine had said, "We must attract pagans to Christ through kindness, but corruption in Christians should be removed by force." What a perfect description of the actions of Bartolomé de las Casas!

The missionary then recalled that two kings of Spain had promulgated laws protecting the Indians, and that Queen Isabella before her death had pleaded for kindness toward the poor Indians. Why had these royal laws and the Queen's plea so often remained dead letters? The bishop's words were so true and his eloquence so moving that again Charles V agreed with him. Again the king decreed new laws favoring the Indians, prohibiting slavery, regulating exploitation of the mines and porterage. Again the missionary had triumphed.

Fr. Bartolomé was now past eighty. Another man would have considered his work done. He had earned a rest. But the missionary could not close his eyes without seeing again the scenes of horror he had known too well: children torn to shreds by hungry dogs, women tortured, men burned alive. He thought of the tropical roads lined with the corpses of Indian porters dead of exhaustion, or Indian villages pillaged and burned. No, his work was not yet done. There were still too many conquistadors bent on continuing their evil ways, of bypassing the laws of God and man.

The news reaching the bishop was not good. In Guatemala, a Franciscan monk who had reprimanded a Spaniard for his cruelty was immediately run out of the country under threat of death. In Peru, despair had driven the Indians to rebellion. In the war of repression that followed, natives were slaughtered by the thousands. The old man had only one desire: to sail again for the New World, where there was so much work still to be done among the wretched Indians for whose salvation he had given his whole life. But his desire was not to be fulfilled. He was nearly paralyzed.

He would never go back again. He would not even get to see his king in England to explain the situation in Peru so that he might try to restrain his trigger-happy military. He did write to England, however. In a moving letter, he pointed out to Charles V that if the Indians had revolted, it was only because more than twenty million of them had been killed, millions more reduced to slavery, and all of them plundered. Once more he cried, "Such behavior brings disgrace to Spain! If evil triumphs, the Christian religion is in peril." Writing from a monastery not far from Madrid, the old man thus used his remaining strength on behalf of his "children."

He died at the age of ninety-two. When the news of his death reached the New World, spontaneous funeral ceremonies were held in hundreds of Indian villages. The Indians felt that they had truly lost a father, and they mourned him with loud, heart-rending cries. The young student of twenty-four who, long years ago, had crossed the sea with Christopher Columbus, dreaming of military victories, of new lands conquered, and of riches quickly won, had found instead another and greater glory. His name was to shine through the ages by the power of love — his love for the downtrodden.

In Bartolomé de las Casas, Spain today venerates one of her noblest figures — intrepid and generous, adventurous and knightly as only the Spanish can be. He had the courage to stand up to his own countrymen who were forgetting the lessons of the Gospel. Few men have been finer witnesses to the charity of Christ.

St. Francis Xavier

∞

Pioneer of Asia

On the sunny morning of August 15, 1534, seven men could be seen hurrying along the rustic road that climbed the Hill of the Martyrs — the Montmartre of the Parisians. One of them limped, an older man, rather scrawny, with a tanned face and eyes like live coals. The six others were all much younger, an incongruous lot, and several of them were certainly foreigners. All of them wore the solemn, resolute expression of men who were about to make a decision of lifelong importance.

They entered the church of the ancient Abbey of Montmartre and went down to the lower chapel, believed to have been built on the very spot where St. Denis, the first Bishop of Paris, was martyred. For a time they prayed. Then the eldest of the group spoke a few words and recited the text of an oath that each of the other six in turn repeated after him. Thus was born a new organization for the service of God, different from a congregation or an order, more like an army of Christ, sworn to fight for Him in any battle. Their gaunt, lame leader was

Ignatius of Loyola, and the vow of Montmartre had just created the Society of Jesus.

Of the six — besides three Spaniards, one Portuguese, and one Savoyard — there was a youth from a country astride the Pyrenees, which had been both French and Spanish, but now seemed to lean more toward France: Navarre, which was also the Basque home of Ignatius himself. His name was Francis Xavier. He was a husky young man, full of energy, with a face that radiated fervor and decision, and also, it must be admitted, told of a stubborn and blunt character. When Ignatius, who usually studied the ground as he talked, raised his eyes to meet those of this young follower, he beamed. "The toughest dough I've ever had the pleasure of kneading," he said.

The founder of the Jesuit order knew Francis Xavier well. For five years they had been together every day, or nearly, from morning to night. Chance — or rather, Providence — had thrown them together as roommates at the St. Barbara College in the slopes of Mount Genevieve, both leading the perennial impecunious life of the eternal student, far richer in ideas and ideals than in coin of the realm. In the beginning, as Ignatius well remembered, Francis was suspicious of him. He was even a little disdainful of the shabby little man who was still a student at forty without having snatched a single degree along the way, the unprepossessing cripple whose lame leg prevented his participation in the games of his comrades. He was no bargain as a roommate. But things were to change radically — and soon.

While Francis, a good Christian destined for the clergy, grumbled impatiently about his family's monetary troubles and his own lack of spending money, Ignatius, who came of equally good stock, accepted his impecunious fate with a smile and a stiff upper lip. Why? Why did Ignatius work his way through college doing menial tasks, practically a mendicant, in fact, without seeming to suffer from the contempt that surrounded him? Francis at last discovered the answer: his comrade's humility was merely the great lesson of Christ, who had also welcomed the role of a man scorned. The example made a great impression on him.

Then, during the long evening arguments, when half a dozen youths crowded into a tiny room to discuss the sublime and the ridiculous, in the eternal manner of the student, and young men of twenty-one became intoxicated on heady ideas and strong concepts, Francis recognized his compatriot from Navarre as a genius, a lucid, vigorous thinker, with his feet solidly planted in earthly reality, but with his head completely possessed by the kingdom of God. Francis had read pages from the book Ignatius was writing. They were solid, penetrating pages that had moved him deeply. And they cemented the friendship between the two men, the young Francis and Ignatius fifteen years his senior, which was to become on the part of Francis a wholehearted relationship of unlimited devotion bordering on veneration.

The founding of the Society of Jesus was a decisive hour for the young man from Navarre, an hour that strikes only once or twice in the lifetime of any man, an hour that, a few minutes later, is beyond recall. In the middle of the sixteenth century, when the Reformation of Luther and Calvin had badly shaken the old citadel of the Mother Church, Ignatius conceived the idea of furnishing the Pope with a supporting militia. The old orders were no longer adequate, and actually some of them stood badly in need of a little reformation themselves. The new society would be bound by an oath of absolute obedience. The Jesuit would be, in the hands of his superiors, "like a cadaver." Wherever the Church was in peril, the new militia of Christ would rush to the rescue.

Years of profound study and meticulous character formation would prepare the Jesuit fathers to act in this manner in the highest intellectual circles, as well as among the humblest, and, elsewhere than in Europe, among the most savage peoples. Dressed as priests, yet living as men of action instead of as cloistered monks, the Jesuits would be forever poised to leap into the breach *ad majorem Dei gloriam* — "for the greater glory of God."

The founder attached importance to one of the many battlefields he had in mind for his new army: the vast lands explored during the preceding century by the great navigators of Spain and Portugal and which stood in such need of another kind of pioneer, the pioneer of Christ. The constitution that Ignatius drew up for the Pope's approval contained a vow obliging a Jesuit to go anywhere the Pope might send him, "either to the Turks or any other infidels whatever, even to that region called India, or to any other heretics or schismatics, as well as to work among the faithful." Such specifications called for men of iron, ready for any eventuality, capable of facing and overcoming any danger and all obstacles.

Francis Xavier, as his old roommate knew, was of this mettle. He would therefore be one of the first Jesuit missionaries.

"May God's will be done, not my own," the young man murmured. He was ordained. He would depart.

∞

The day after the ceremony of Montmartre, the seven friends decided to leave for Italy to present themselves to the Pope and receive his approbation. They went on foot, telling their beads as they walked, begging their bread, and stopping to address crowds in every village marketplace — crowds, incidentally, that often made fun of their foreign accents. Francis did not often speak, but when he did, everyone recognized the effectiveness of his living eloquence.

They stayed a long time in Venice, where they devoted themselves to serving the poor wretches in the hospital for incurables, swabbing ulcers, sweeping out filth, and breathing the stench of the dying. Francis stayed in Bologna with a friend while his companions went on to Rome. Here he carried on his works of charity and preaching with such assiduous devotion that his health gave way. Burned up by fever, he wasted away to a skeleton.

And despite the many conversions he had made in all parts of the city, he was still dissatisfied. He thought of the vast spaces of the world where the Word of Christ had still not penetrated. In Venice, he had been moved to pity by the sight of the slaves that wealthy patricians had bought and imported from Ethiopia and Arabia. One night, he dreamed that he was carrying one of the slaves on his back, carrying him toward the Light of Christ. He needed only an opportunity for his missionary vocation to be confirmed.

Heroes of God

The opportunity was not long in coming. Francis Xavier was in Rome, recuperating from his illness — his friends had given him up for dead — when the King of Portugal, having heard of the new militia of Christ, asked Ignatius for two of his fathers for the Portuguese colonies in India. Xavier's heart rejoiced, but his chief refused to let him go; he was still too weak for such an adventure. Providence, however, was on his side. One of the two Jesuit fathers chosen to go was taken seriously ill, and it was necessary to replace him, because the Portuguese ambassador was anxious to leave for Lisbon and wanted to take the Jesuit contingent with him. Francis Xavier was chosen as an alternate.

So he left for Portugal with little baggage but with immense hope in his heart. Ten months later, on April 7, 1541, his thirty-fifth birthday, he sailed aboard the *Santiago* — the St. James — with two other fathers and the new Governor General of Portuguese India.

The Portuguese colonial empire at this time was of great extent and prestige. From Lisbon to the Cape of Good Hope, from the Cape to India, from India to Malacca, from Indochina to Japan, there was no port of importance that did not interest the Portuguese. Their trade was more than flourishing. From Mozambique, they took gold dust and ivory; from Muscat and Oman on the Persian Gulf, they shipped the goods of Central Asia. Goa, Ceylon, and Nagapatam were open doors to the treasures of India. Through Malacca and the Malay Peninsula, they traded with Indochina. In the Moluccas, they established trading posts for the Spice Islands. Macao, near Canton, was the Portuguese center for commerce with China and Japan.

It is difficult to conceive how such a small nation was able in less than half a century to dominate with its military and trading posts a seaboard of some eleven thousand miles. Love of money alone was not enough to explain this remarkable display of energy. Also important was heroic patriotism and religious fervor such as the desire to serve God in the far lands, like that which filled the heart of the young Navarrese in the service of the Portuguese king when he set sail for Goa, the capital of the Portuguese colonial empire.

It was a long, hard journey. Ordinarily a fast sailing ship could turn the Cape, call at Mozambique for supplies, and reach India in six months, but headwinds and violent storms alternating with dead calms prolonged the passage to thirteen months. And what a passage! There were epidemics aboard. Fights broke out among the little sample of humanity huddled together for too long in the cramped quarters of the merchantman. Knives were drawn and blasphemies echoed.

Francis Xavier went to work among the wretched emigrants and the Ethiopian slaves of the sailors, sick and sweltering on the overcrowded decks, gasping for breath in the unbearable tropical heat. He resumed the mission of kindness and mercy he had begun so successfully in the Italian cities. He preached, too, not only aboard ship, but in every port of call. His fire was contagious. By the time the ship reached India, the crew thought the world of him.

Francis Xavier went ashore in the capital of Portuguese India on May 6, 1542, in the company of the new viceroy. He carried credentials from the Pope naming him Apostolic Nonce and giving him power to reform or redress whatever he deemed necessary. The pompous colonials were disappointed in him. At Goa, as at other trading posts, the colonials lived only for luxury, for gold and precious stones, for soft living made softer by dozens of slaves. Even the Portuguese clergy had grown somewhat flabby in the free-and-easy atmosphere of colonial indolence. All expected to see the ambassador of the Pope arrive in full regalia and hold court with some glitter and ceremony. They were surprised and not too pleased when the Nonce hurried directly to the hospital and with his own hands tended the less savory patients, heard their confessions, and gave them the sacraments. They were even less pleased when he visited the prisons, swarming with vermin and jammed with a malodorous mixture of convicts and slaves, thugs and thieves. They even heard that he planned to visit the leper camp outside the city, without fear of catching the terrible malady.

This marvelous Christian attitude of charity and humility did more good than dozens of fine sermons and visits to the powerful. The sick, the aged, the destitute, ragged children — all the little people sang the praises of the new priest. He performed more baptisms in a month than Goa had seen in a year. The needy natives whom he baptized crowded to hear him preach at the sound of his bell in the streets, and his clarion appeal: "Come, friends of Jesus Christ. Send your sons and your daughters. Send your slaves to hear the Holy Doctrine, for the love of God."

He had begun by teaching the catechism in one small chapel; it was not long before it was taught in the churches of Goa. The Portuguese clergy, distrustful at first, was not long in following his example. Something had changed; there was no doubt about it.

For five months, Francis continued this routine, but useful as it was, it was not enough. It was not for the purpose of reminding the Portuguese of the precepts of the Gospel that he had come to the East. The vocation to which God had summoned him was to bring light to those still in the shadow. His task in the East was to do what St. Martin had done in the countryside of Gaul: overthrow the idols, uproot superstition. And he was off!

On the southwest coast of India, from Travancore to Cape Comorin, where the pearl fishers dove for their treasure, there were little nuclei of Christians who had undergone quick Baptism by some passing priest but who knew nothing whatever of Christianity and who still lived like pagans. They had to be started again from the beginning; they did not even know the catechism. Francis Xavier set out for this coast, stopping at every village, indefatigable, patient, every inch a saint.

It was not a simple task. The frightful heat, followed by the monsoon rains, which in an hour transformed rivers into oceans and roads into lakes of mud, did not make for easy travel. The language difficulty was great; languages varied from region to region, so it was impossible to speak directly to the natives. As Francis Xavier was far from a gifted linguist, he was forced to rely on interpreters, who might well twist his thoughts to suit themselves. For a man of his frail constitution, his life was a grueling one: eating strange foods, if at all, sleeping in odd places or in the open air, at the constant mercy of voracious insects, the threat of poisonous snakes, the alarming rustle of bats' wings. But the worst of all was the intrigue and distrust of both the Portuguese colonials and the Indian priests and lay leaders.

The apostolate of Francis Xavier was of necessity addressed to the lower classes. It was well known that Hindu Society was rigidly divided into absolutely hermetically sealed castes, from the Pariahs, the Untouchables, on the bottom to the Brahmans at the top. The Brahmans kept the lesser peoples in a state of systematic ignorance, allowing them only a ration of superstition and vulgar rites. The attitude of the Brahmans toward the Christian missionaries, who treated all men as brothers, could therefore hardly be other than one of suspicion.

The greatest joys of Fr. Xavier came to him from the humble, the little people, to whom he quickly explained in simple terms the fundamental law of Christianity, the law of love and of universal brotherhood. Those who heard him rushed to be baptized in amazing numbers. His results were little short of prodigious. In Travancore, for example, in southwestern India, to which he tramped on foot, quietly and without fuss, he made more conversions in thirty days than the Portuguese clergy, richly dressed and sumptuously lodged, had made in thirty years of travel by horse and carriage. True fidelity to the spirit of Christ was indeed a great power.

The greatest sorrows of Fr. Xavier, and his greatest indignation, came from the attitude of the Portuguese and other European colonials who, supposedly Christians, were far from faithful to the Christian spirit. The violence and injustice with which they treated the unarmed natives revolted his soul to saintly anger. Whenever he saw the natives mistreated or tortured, he always protested to the masters. When he saw rascally merchants cheating the Indians, trading worthless trinkets and inferior materials for gold and ivory and precious stones, he never hesitated to speak his mind. Many times he wrote to John III, King of Portugal, begging him to intervene on the side of justice, but he was never sure that his letters had been delivered. In any case, they had no effect. The colonials continued to exploit the natives, hand in hand with Arab traders and slave dealers. The heart of the missionary bled for their victims.

To be a spokesman for Christ and a conqueror for the Holy Spirit is a rigid and never-ending ordeal. Men are men, and the mere act of Baptism is not enough to change them. The effort must always be recommenced; the ground gained must be, not only defended, but reconquered. At the southern end of the Coromandel Coast of southeastern India, across a narrow arm of the sea, there lay a happy, luxuriant island of which Francis Xavier had longed dreamed: Ceylon. Into this green and mountainous land, sacred to Hindu, Buddhist, and Moslem alike, Francis Xavier had sent several native priests, for his plan had been from the first to ordain natives to aid him in his apostolate. But a frightful tragedy was to crush this budding Christianity. Fearing that the evangelization of his people was a Portuguese plot to undermine his authority, the Rajah ordered a massacre of everyone who had been baptized. There were no fewer than five hundred martyrs!

But a man of God does not allow himself to be cast down by apparent failure. His concern is not so much the little that has been done, but the immense work still left to be done. Always forward! Beyond the vast southern seas stretched new lands awaiting the missionaries.

Francis Xavier set sail again. Full-rigged merchantmen and miserable junk: all were his vehicles in reaching for the unknown. It would take more pages than is possible to spare here merely to follow the tracks of this tireless traveler. Here he was in Malaya in 1545, after a fearful crossing in which the ship came so near to foundering that the captain himself was in tears. In Malacca, a cosmopolitan city of Chinese, Burmans, Ethiopians, and Polynesians, he resumed his old role of catechist and nurse to the humble, without neglecting the opportunity of bringing to God an occasional wealthy trader or powerful captain. Next he turned up — by accident — in the Moluccas, far, very far away to the north of the Sunda Islands, where he landed when blown off his course by contrary winds. Here he reclaimed in the name of Christ the Alfuros of Amboina, who had turned Christian for hate of the Arabs, but who knew nothing of their supposed religion; the savages of Ternate Island; and finally, the worst of the lot, the pirates and bandits of Morotai, who were cannibals as well.

This was the life that made Francis Xavier completely happy. His feet bled from long months on impossible trails. He was often tortured by fever and rheumatism. He was constantly surrounded by danger: hostile climate, men, beasts, erupting volcanoes. But nothing mattered to him except the task to which he had devoted himself, body and soul. During his three months in the Moluccas, he had baptized hundreds and hundreds of natives. In that fact lay his reward and his happiness.

∞

It was in Malacca, on his return from the Moluccas, that the saint heard of a new country that might prove a field for his apostolate. The second period of his glorious story was about to begin. After India and the Indies, Japan.

One day while he was celebrating Mass, two men came into the chapel. One was a Portuguese whom he recognized as an old friend. The other was a stranger — a thin little dark-complexioned man in a brown robe, carrying a sword with a lacquered scabbard. His name was Yagiro. He was Japanese, and he had crossed many leagues of ocean to find the missionary. He had heard of Francis Xavier from sailors and traders, for there were few ports in the Far East where his name and virtues were not known and glorified. Yagiro was a gentle, cautious man, with the traditional politeness of the Japanese. He spoke at length of his country, describing to the missionary its fine scenery, its climate, and its flowers; but he spoke mostly of his compatriots, who he said were intelligent, courageous, and much interested in religious questions.

The missionary took this visit as a sign from Heaven. A few European traders had penetrated these happy isles, but from a Christian point of view, they were virgin territory. Since the Lord had so clearly indicated the work to be done, Francis Xavier would go to Japan. "Within two years," he told Yagiro, "I will bring the Word of God to your country."

The missionary prepared his expedition with great care. This man of courage, this Adventurer of God, was certainly no madcap. Quite the opposite. He knew exactly how to plan ahead, how to bring his projects to fruition by nurturing them in great detail. Patiently he questioned every trader he could find who had been to Japan. He gradually compiled a thick dossier of geographical and sociological information on the island nation and sent a resume to his superiors in the Society of Jesus, asking their advice. He realized that he would be embarking on a venture more daring than any he had yet undertaken. He would be without the protection of Portuguese guns in case of peril. No matter. Danger was of no importance. Obstacles were of no importance.

He would sail. And he did sail, on June 24, 1549.

The journey from Malaya to Japan was fantastic. The Chinese junk that he had chartered was a miserable patchwork of second-hand parts and was scarcely seaworthy. The crew burned hundreds of joss sticks before the idol installed in a niche on the quarterdeck, without result. The junk still ran into a violent typhoon that nearly sent her to the bottom; an epidemic decimated the crew; and the captain insisted on taking the long way around by way of China. Neither did the idol prevent the captain's daughter (who came aboard for reasons never quite clear) from falling overboard and being crushed to death against the hull by a huge wave. It took all the apostle's patience and energy to nurse the craft and crew through to Japan, by August.

The missionary found the country in a sad state. The long fight between the imperial court and the shoguns, the military governors who had displaced the Mikado for all practical purposes, had reduced Japan to a state of anarchy. The provincial lords had become independent rulers in their own domains, much as in feudal France before the Capetian dynasty established unity and order. Human life was cheap, depending upon the whim of a captain, a minor functionary, or a bandit. Buddhist monasteries had been transformed into fortresses where adventurers and black sheep of good families might take refuge. Perhaps an unimportant missionary who worked without ostentation might go unnoticed in this chaos, but his task would not be easy.

St. Francis Xavier was to remain in Japan for two years. He had probably landed there with the intention of spending his life there, of creating a living Christianity on Japanese soil; but Providence evidently intended for him to do no more than sow the seed, leaving the harvest for others who would come after him. A letter from St. Ignatius, his chief, which finally reached him after many months in transit, notified him that he had been named Provincial Father of the Indies for the Society of Jesus and ordered him to return to Goa. He complied, but not before he had inaugurated his apostolate and broken ground for future sowings.

He had landed on Kyushu, the southernmost of the larger Japanese islands, where he lived for several months in Kagoshima. The local feudal lord — "The Duke," Francis Xavier called him — received him with friendly respect and accepted with interest his numerous presents, including a picture of the Virgin and the Infant Jesus. The good Yagiro, the merchant who had persuaded him to come to Japan, acted as his interpreter. He entered many Japanese homes, spoke freely of his Faith, and even discussed religion with numerous bonzes, or Buddhist priests. He began to win converts, especially among the little people, and the tireless baptist was soon happily hard at work, almost as successfully as he had been in Travancore.

But his success was too great to last. Jealous of the growing influence of the new Christians, the Buddhist priests went to the Daimyo, the lord of Kagoshima, with alarmist stories. The Daimyo, who had expected that his welcome of the missionary would be followed by the arrival of Portuguese commerce, lent a friendly ear. While he did not expel the men of God, he tolerated demonstrations against them, and he forbade his subjects to embrace the Christian Faith. Too late! The group who had been baptized had already dispersed throughout the country.

Francis Xavier had heard much about the most beautiful city of Japan: Kyoto, a city of ninety thousand houses, the glorious capital of the Mikado, where more than 3,500 students attended five universities. He decided he would have a look at Kyoto before returning to India, and sow a few handfuls of evangelical seed. He set off across regions wracked by civil war, traveling sometimes by sea, more often many footsore miles by land. He was admitted to Japanese homes with the hospitality characteristic of the country, held long conversations with his hosts, answered numerous questions, and spoke of his religion, of Christ and His message. His route was marked with baptisms. He also learned much about the country and its customs, so that his letters are certainly the first serious documentation on Japan known to the West. He covered more than five hundred difficult and sometimes painful miles on the road to Kyoto, but he was sustained by a great idea. He would see the emperor and speak to him of Christ. If he could persuade the emperor himself to become a Christian, would not the whole country ask to be baptized?

He was due for a great disappointment. When he entered Kyoto one bitter, snowy January day of 1551, he found that the fabled, much-vaunted capital was little more than a ghost town. The city had been laid waste by fire, ruined by the civil war. Looters roamed the streets, and banditry flourished in broad daylight. Pagodas were crumbling, and the imperial palace itself was badly dilapidated. He realized that it would be futile to pursue a chimera.

Returning to India, he took up his new tasks as Provincial Father. He had to restore order in the College of Goa, where the young recruits sent out by the Society of Jesus were not getting along very well together. He also resumed his patient work as a catechist, even though he had little time to spare. He was constantly exhorting the local Portuguese clergy, as well as his fellow Jesuits, that they must not only spread the Word of Christ, but that they must themselves be faithful to it.

But administrative work was ill-suited to a man of action who was also a man of iron. He grew restless. He dreamed of a new apostolate. People had spoken to him of China. He must go and have a look. The seed must be sown in China, too.

After many arguments and vexations, he was finally authorized to sail for China. His little ship, the *Santa Croce* — "Holy Cross" — touched at Singapore en route to Canton. The Pearl River, which led to the great South China metropolis, was swarming with pirates and smugglers of all nationalities. The ship managed to make port safely, but the long, hard journey was the culmination of the many wearing adverse factors of a wandering life upon a frail constitution. At the moment of going ashore, Francis Xavier was gripped by a debilitating fever.

To the fathers who carried him to the small boat that was taking him to land, he murmured, "Let us all meet again at God's Judgment Seat." He did not give up hope, however. Perhaps some Chinese merchantman would take him aboard and carry him farther, very much farther, in the service of the Christ.

But the weather was growing cold, and provisions were getting scarce. A Portuguese sailor found him one day shivering with fever beside the road leading to some wretched family to whom he was carrying clothing. The sailor called a doctor who, according to the customs of the time, bled him. This was too much for Francis. Weak from the loss of blood, he fainted. They brought him to, tried to feed him. He fainted again and again.

During his lucid moments, he spoke of God and of Christ, exhorting all who heard him to be faithful. He prayed. A poor Hindu from the Malabar Coast and a Chinese man he had baptized were his sole companions in his supreme hour. Even they became insolent when they realized Francis was dying, probably getting ready to rifle his belongings.

"How great is my suffering," murmured the saint.

He died on November 27, 1552, at the age of forty-six.

∞

Thus ended a prodigiously full life, every hour of which was devoted to God, from the day he first sailed from Europe to the day of his obscure death on the distant shores of Asia. How are we to understand this man, this traveler for Christ, whose ceaseless activity and perpetual wanderings are astonishingly reminiscent of the first soldiers of the Holy Spirit — a St. Paul, first of all; or a St. Martin, Apostle to the Gauls; or later, when the Church was converting the barbarians of the West, a St. Columba, a St. Amand, or a St. Boniface? He had within him much of the enterprise and spirit of adventure that during the preceding century had sent men out from the Iberian Peninsula to explore the unknown paths of the wide world. The man to whom France, Spain, and Portugal may lay equal claim — does he not bring to mind a Christopher Columbus, a Vasco da Gama, or a Jacques Cartier? Yet his love of daring voyages was dedicated to Christ and the service of the Church, for he succeeded in subjugating his other identities: the proud gentleman of Navarre and the lofty and erudite student. He used their special qualities for the sole glory of God.

His methods of baptizing the pagans have caused some comment. Some of his biographers claim that he baptized 1,200,000 natives in ten years, which comes to 329 a day. This is obviously quite a figure, and we must allow for the possibility of exaggeration. Yet Francis himself records the baptism of ten thousand persons in Travancore in one month, admitting that his arms were very tired. Assuredly baptisms of this sort without much preparation of the baptized could not have been very sound.

That is why the Christian communities founded by St. Francis Xavier in Asia could not long survive their founder. Less than thirty years after his death, the fall of Portuguese

India into Spanish hands brought about the partial liquidation of his churches, which were later attacked by the Moslems and also by the Protestant missionaries. And yet in Travancore and elsewhere in India, there are still today faithful Catholic Christians who are the direct result of the work of the great missionary.

The same story was repeated in Japan. Although the Catholic communities there were subjected to frightful persecution in 1613 — Jesuit priests were crucified, and uncounted Christians were arrested, tortured, and killed — a sturdy Christian core has survived to this day to allow the tree of the Church to put down new roots, to grow, and to become truly important.

Francis Xavier was a pioneer, a trailblazer for God. Without bothering too much about consolidating his conquests, he pressed ever forward, penetrating hostile lands, cutting a path, sowing the good seed, and leaving the harvest to God. The thing that matters most in the service of the Lord is not immediate results, but to bear witness. Only the future can tell whether these heroic lives and sacrifices have been useful, and the future is in the hands of God.

St. Isaac Jogues

∞

Slave of the Iroquois

Early in September of 1636, an impressive flotilla of canoes paddled up the St. Lawrence River into Canada. The sentinels of the Algonquin tribes gave no alarm as they watched them pass: the Hurons were on their way home after having sold their furs to the whites, bringing back in exchange firearms, medicines, provisions, and trinkets. This was obviously not an expedition of war. The tomahawk had not been thrown across the tribal boundaries. The Algonquins let the Hurons pass.

But their curiosity was aroused. The Indian paddlers were not alone. A strange white man sat among the stalwart bronzed bodies striped with multicolor grease and sparkling with ornaments of copper and seashells. The stranger was not the thin old white man the Hurons had brought through several weeks earlier. He was young, husky, sharp-featured, and rosy-cheeked. He was dressed, of course, the same way as the others. Why did the whites rig themselves out in those ridiculously uncomfortable long, black gowns when they came to visit the tribes? But wasn't everything the whites did strange and baffling?

Heroes of God

The Black Robes had been coming to live in the Great Forest for some years now. They lived like the Indians, with a few exceptions: they didn't kill, they didn't steal, and they had no wives. The medicine men hated them, declaring that their very presence drew the anger of the Invisible Powers in the form of epidemics and cataclysms. Notwithstanding, here and there some Indian would accept the religion of these alien priests who had come from so far away; but they were few, far between, and not viewed with favor.

But the Black Robes were persistent. When one of them fell sick or was killed, another took his place at once. So, in place of the wraithlike figure the canoes had taken down to Trois-Rivières earlier, they were bringing back this husky fellow who seemed surprised by nothing. For sixteen days, he had been crouching on his heels, oblivious of the shrill whine of mosquitoes, the burning noonday sun, and the penetrating cold of night, moving his lips slightly as he read almost constantly from a black book. During portages around the rapids, he lent a hand in carrying the pirogues through miles of reeds and thickets, never complaining. The Hurons liked him.

Thus did Fr. Isaac Jogues of the Society of Jesus reach the post assigned to him by his superiors at Trois-Rivières: Ihonatiria, "The Hamlet Overlooking the Loaded Canoes," a small cluster of huts topping a peninsula in Lake Huron. He was twenty-nine years old when the order came to join the annual convoy to the tribes. He thanked God with all the fervor of his youth for having granted his wish.

For years he had vowed to consecrate himself to the Lord. He had been one of those children of exemplary zeal who had been praised for his perfect obedience since the age of nine or ten. When his father or his teacher had been forced to correct him — for he had been a lively, passionate, rather wild boy — he had often kissed the hand that punished him. At the college of the Fathers in Orleans he was an intelligent, studious, retentive youth with a great sense of curiosity, and soon attracted the attention of the educators. At this school where men had but one aim, where men strove neither for money nor position, where nothing mattered but the glory of God and the salvation of human souls, Isaac had quickly found his vocation. He would become a Jesuit and, like Francis Xavier, who had been canonized in 1622 when young Jogues was about sixteen, a Jesuit missionary.

That is why on an autumn day of 1636, he found himself springing ashore, stretching his long legs, numb from having been folded under him in a canoe for so long, and surveying his future catechumens with some amazement. One of them had black cheeks, a red nose, and the rest of his face painted a bright blue. Another was half black, half white. A third was covered from shins to forehead with multicolored stripes, circles, and zigzags. Most of them had parallel furrows cut into their hair, with the intervening ridges standing stiff and black like the bristles on a wild boar's head. It was this appearance, in fact, that led the French missionaries to call the Indians "Hurons" — from the French word for boar's head, *hure*.

But what the Lord proposes is always delightful. Young Jogues remembered the words of his venerated master, Fr. Louis Lallement, a true man of God: "Brother Isaac, you will die nowhere else but in Canada." Isaac Jogues had accepted his destiny with joy in his heart.

Canada! Under the impetus given by the great Cardinal de Richelieu, Canada had for the past ten years been the dream of French youth. Although, since the death of Henri IV, French efforts to gain a foothold in the new lands of America had been only half-hearted — even the valiant Champlain had been satisfied to consolidate his hold on Quebec and to clear the surrounding territory — Richelieu had seen into the future with a clear eye. Under his patronage, the Company of the Hundred Associates had since 1627 been transporting settlers to the New World with a guarantee of three years' maintenance. The French population in Canada continued to grow despite the capture of Quebec by the English in 1629 and the death in harness of Champlain in 1635.

Canada! How many hearts burned with Canadian ardor, from court to cloisters, from school to society! Men and women, priests and soldiers, even nuns, dreamed of sailing for the great lonely spaces, some drawn by the love of money, others by the love of God.

Among the latter were many Jesuits. Never a year went by without its novitiates turning out as young fathers anxious to carry on the Christian mission in far-off lands and add a page of glory to mission history. It was because of the Jesuits that Montreal would someday become a great metropolis. But in the seventeenth century, they worked in the wilderness. Fr. Le Jeune worked zealously among the Algonquins north of the St. Lawrence between the Atlantic and the Great Lakes. The Hurons, further to the east, between the lake bearing their name and Lake Ontario, were served by several missions directed by Fr. de Brébeuf, a giant of a man, and frail Fr. Garnier. Only the Iroquois, south of Lake Ontario and Lake Erie, seemed inaccessible to the Jesuits. Whether they were Mohawks, Senecas, Oneidas, or Cayugas, they were hostile toward the French, partly because of their warlike nature, partly because they were stirred up by the English and the Dutch.

Fr. Isaac Jogues climbed the bank behind the Indian carrying his meager baggage and followed the steep path to the cluster of huts that was the village. He turned for a moment to look behind him at the immense freshwater sea stretching out its gray-and-blue expanse to the misty horizon. To his right and left, the infinite forest, rusty with autumn, crowded upon the shore. From the marshes came the loud nostalgic croaking of the bullfrogs. This was the place to which God had called him.

∞

The life of a missionary in Canada in the early part of the seventeenth century, in which heroism was an everyday matter, is difficult to imagine. The life of every spokesman for Christ is obviously difficult and dangerous always, but today even the most distant post in the heart of Africa or in the islands of the Pacific has a modicum of comfort, the protection of public powers, medicines, and a radio. Such modest conveniences were, of course, unknown in North America three centuries ago.

Every day was an adventure for the missionary. In summer, he crossed forests by lakes and rivers, paddling interminably up dangerous streams, interrupted by backbreaking portages, menaced by wolves and bears or, more insidiously, by fever-carrying insects. In winter, there were long journeys by sleigh in extreme cold, through blizzards of violent wind, overnight stops in a hole in the snow, with the risk of getting lost through the perfidy or stupidity of a guide, to be found again, as was Fr. Anne de Noüe, kneeling in the snow, bareheaded, arms crossed upon his breast, his eyes open and looking to Heaven, frozen to death.

Sojourns in the villages were no less perilous or more satisfying. The Indian huts of bark and skins stretched on poles gave paltry shelter. One corner would serve as chapel; the rest, a single room, would serve as kitchen and dormitory, dining room and workshop. A pile of bark chips covered with a mat would do for sleeping. The primitive hearth gave off an eternal cloud of acrid smoke. No linen, no change of clothing. For food, there was an Indian porridge of stone-ground corn seasoned with bits of dried fish, or venison that had been trampled with bare feet (and had an accumulation of dust, feathers, and nameless debris ground into it), then dried until it took on the texture of boot leather. Instructions to Jesuit missionaries specified that they must "eat the food of the natives without showing disgust or repugnance." O sacred virtue of obedience!

However, these material difficulties were among the lesser evils that the missionary encountered during his apostolate. The Hurons might overwhelm him with their lack of modesty and their vermin, but what was really frightful and frightening was their sneaking distrust, their cruelty always ready to burst forth, and the abrupt, fuming anger that could overtake even those who seemed the most faithful, set off by the word of a witch doctor exploiting some epidemic or unfortunate accident. One of the most heroic missionaries of the time, Fr. Jerome Lalemant, once wrote, "We would rather be hit on the head with a hatchet than go on year after year living this life we must live here daily, working to convert barbarians."

Fr. Isaac Jogues lived this life for nearly seven years. Obeying the precept of St. Paul, prince of missionaries, he became a Huron among Hurons,[17] in his effort to bring them to Christ. He slept in hovels with hair-raising odors, sharing the space not only with Indians, but with dogs and swine. He shared meals with the head of the family who, to honor his guest, would toss him a hunk of jerked venison, right from a boiling pot, as if he were throwing a bone to a dog. He perfected himself in the difficult Huron language, which has only eight consonants and reduces words to inarticulate grunts.

Yet life was bearable in the beginning at Ihonatiria, because there were eleven white men in the little community of St. Joseph nearby, six of whom were priests. But the needs of the apostolate were not to leave the little group intact for long. Fr. de Brébeuf, the superior, decided to proselytize the Tetons who lived west of the Great Lakes, far to the west, and about whom little was known. He sent Fr. Isaac Jogues and three other missionaries to the west to establish a station there.

The years that followed were one continuous heroic effort, a life of high adventure and obscure devotion, of hardships and drama. Living so long among the Indians, Fr. Jogues grew

[17] The French word *huron*, spelled with a lowercase *h* means "a boor." — TRANS.

to resemble those he was trying to evangelize. His strength, his nimbleness, and his endurance amazed them. No Indian could beat him in a foot race, and he was their equal with a canoe paddle. His face had become bronzed, his cheeks hollow and hard. *"Ondessonk,"* the Indians called him: "Bird of prey."

What were the results of his six years of work? Not much, on the surface — 120 worthy to be called baptized, a mere handful. Among them there were no doubt a few true Christians who had heard and understood the message of the Savior and who would be His witnesses among their brothers. But compared with this accomplishment, what a huge task remained to be done! How many Huron souls there were still to be saved, and what dark and sullied souls they were still! Despite all that the missionaries might say, the lives of these unfortunates continued for the most part to consist of nothing but lust, violence, and rapine. They remained in the grip of the worst superstitions, and the precepts of the Gospel were futile against Indian belief in the manitous, evil spirits to which they made bloody sacrifices. Worse yet, the missionaries knew that their Indians still practiced cannibalism on occasion, cutting out the heart of a brave enemy and devouring it to assimilate his courage.

How were such accumulations of errors to be overcome? Like all men pursuing a grand design, Fr. Jogues held of small account the things he had already accomplished. He dreamed only of the work still to be done. And that work was immense, overwhelming.

During the long hours he spent in prayer before the ciborium of his sorry little chapel, he begged God to guide him.

Slave of the Iroquois

Since experience had proved that only the blood of martyrs could cause the good seed of the Gospel to grow in barren soil, he asked the All-Powerful to accept his own, offering it with all his heart for the conversion of his cherished savages. One night he experienced an ecstasy. It was not the first, for Christ had already spoken to him several times before. The voice of the Master resounded mysteriously in his ears, saying, "Thy prayers are granted. It shall happen as thou hast asked. Take heart! Be valiant!"

The progress of Christianity among the Hurons had increased the traditional hate borne them by the Iroquois. During the summer of 1642, war broke out between the two peoples. There were war dances around the campfires. Tomahawks were brandished to the beat of death chants. Lightning raids by the Mohawks left villages in flames. From the Great Lakes to the Atlantic, the countryside was aroused.

Fr. Jogues was faced with a difficult decision. Under these conditions, should he undertake his regular annual journey to market with his furs? It would mean traveling five hundred miles through hostile country. Yet without the European provisions and the ammunition he would bring back in return for his pelts, how would the mission live and defend itself during the coming year? The expedition would set out as usual.

Fr. Jogues would be the leader, accompanied by Fr. Raymbault, whose health required that he return to the city, by three French laymen who were serving the mission fathers, and by some twenty picked Hurons, all Christians, led by

Chief Eustace. The members of the departing expedition smoked a final calumet with those staying behind, passing the peace pipe from mouth to mouth. Then the canoes pushed off, the paddles flashing rhythmically in the sun.

The journey downstream went smoothly enough, except that normal fatigue was increased by the presence of Fr. Raymbault, who was so weak that he had to be helped over the portages. The expedition stopped at Trois-Rivières, then paddled on to Quebec.

The return trip saw an augmented flotilla, for twenty other Hurons had joined the expedition, as well as another Frenchman, a big-hearted young man named René Goupil who had offered to place his knowledge of medicine at the disposition of the missionaries. The Jesuits stopped at Trois-Rivières on July 31, 1642, to celebrate St. Ignatius' Day, and then the twelve canoes pushed off into the broad expanse of the St. Lawrence for the trip upstream. The first day they paddled more than thirty miles. Soon after their departure at dawn of the second day, keen-eyed Huron scouts discovered disquieting signs in the mud of the riverbanks: bare footprints and marks where canoes had been beached. The Iroquois were near at hand.

An instant later, they attacked. The early-morning calm was shattered by war whoops of the Mohawks, the most savage of the Iroquois tribes. They broke through the undergrowth, frightful figures smeared with red war paint. Shots rang out from muskets furnished by the Dutch. The first six canoes were raked by gunfire. The Hurons of the other six jumped overboard and swam for shore, trying to escape. Of the five white men, young Goupil was hit, the three French laymen had disappeared, and Fr. Jogues found himself alone among the reeds that lined the bank, tall reeds that hid him completely. He was safe.

Another man would have praised God for protecting him and would have remained hidden until his enemies had gone off. But not Fr. Jogues. "The idea of flight appalled me," he was to write later. "Could I possibly, I asked myself, desert my Frenchmen and my poor savages without giving them the aid that the Church of my God had entrusted to me? My body must die its transitory death in order for me to achieve life everlasting." And walking from his hiding place, he gave himself up to the Iroquois.

The horror began immediately. One of the French laymen, a man named Couture, returning to the scene of battle, walked into the sights of a Mohawk musket. Quickly the Frenchman raised his own musket and fired. The Indian fell dead. At once the Mohawks swarmed into the reeds, surrounded Couture and Fr. Jogues, beat them, and dragged them to dry land. The Indians then began tearing out their fingernails, one by one. With their sharpened teeth, they bit into the quick, chewing the tips of the index fingers until the bone showed through. Only fear of a counterattack interrupted this abominable scene. The Mohawks threw their prisoners into canoes and shoved off. They had captured nineteen Hurons and three Frenchmen. Fr. Jogues lay at the bottom of a pirogue, where he had been thrown like a bundle of pelts. He prayed and meditated.

Was his hour of martyrdom near?

The life of the unfortunate prisoners during the days to follow can scarcely be described. Whenever the Mohawks came to one of their own villages, they treated the tribesmen to the finest spectacle imaginable: the torture of the missionaries. They made them run the gauntlet — hurry between two rows of Indians who beat them with switches. They hoisted them to a platform to be pilloried. They hung them from gibbets by the arms. Should one of them faint, as did Isaac Jogues, the Indians brought him to by holding a flaming brand to his thighs or by burning a finger. When his wounds seemed to be healing, they raked them open again with their fingernails.

All the Christians, whites and Indians alike, bore the torture with superhuman courage. Fr. Jogues did not open his lips. Only once did he flinch — when he was forced to watch the torture of his Indian friend Chief Eustace. They had cut off the Chief's thumbs and driven pointed sticks into the wounds until the points came out at the elbows. It is a wonder that these martyrs survived such barbarous treatment, yet they did without one cry of pain.

One day the three surviving Frenchmen were walking at the rear of the file, which was not well guarded. "Run, Goupil," Fr. Jogues whispered to the young medical student. "You and Couture have a chance of getting away. I'll stay behind."

"Never!" the young man replied. "Your fate shall be mine. And if we survive, I vow that I myself will join the Society of Jesus."

Four times, five, six times the sinister series of tortures was repeated, with frightful variations according to the savage whim of the torturer. One day when Fr. Jogues had been hanging by the armpits for a quarter of an hour, he was heard to murmur in his distress the words uttered by Jesus on the cross: "My God, my God, why hast Thou forsaken me?"[18] Another day the Mohawks found it amusing to force a woman prisoner, an Algonquin Christian, to cut off one of the fingers of the missionary. Terrified, she succeeded on her second trial. Promptly Fr. Jogues stooped to pick up his own flesh from the ground and flung it far away so that the Algonquin woman would not be forced to eat it. At last, one April night, the prisoners were told they would be burned alive the next evening.

The execution did not take place. The Iroquois were divided into two parties: the Bear Tribe, which was the war party, and the Wolf Tribe, which was the peace party, favoring peaceful trade with the whites. To burn three white men, the Wolves argued, would merely invite reprisals. There were rumors that the French governor was already readying a rescue expedition. Cooler heads prevailed, and Jogues and his companions were allowed to live. However, they were presented to Mohawk chiefs as slaves. The three most important Christian Hurons captured were not so fortunate. Chiefs Eustace, Stephen, and Paul died bravely — burned at the stake.

The dismal captivity of the three Frenchmen dragged on for months and months, with humiliation piled on humiliation, torment on torment. Starved, weakened by disease, the white slaves were pitiful servants. They would have been liquidated long since, had not the news spread from tepee to tepee that the white men in the cities, as well as in the outposts,

[18] Matt. 27:46.

were aware of the missionaries' existence. Some Dutch traders had told the authorities at New Amsterdam (today New York) about the strange white slaves held by the Mohawks, and an envoy had come upstate to make a personal investigation. The Indians' bargaining position, in the meantime, had been weakened by a reverse at Fort Richelieu, a new French outpost, where an Iroquois attack had been thrown back with heavy losses. Soon afterward a Dutchman was allowed to talk to the slaves; he offered to pay six hundred florins for their ransom.

All this conciliatory talk enraged the Bears. One day some of these extremists found young René Goupil teaching a young Indian child to make the Sign of the Cross. Immediately they fell upon Goupil and, before the horrified eyes of Fr. Jogues, killed him with tomahawks. Jogues thought his hour had come, but he was wrong. God still needed him. The Indians merely turned him over to the worst enemy of the Christians, the chief who had ordered the missionary's finger to be cut off.

Even in this predicament, the calm and serenity of Fr. Jogues prevailed over his captors. The sister of the sinister chief, who was greatly respected by her tribe, took the father under her protection. "My nephew," she called him. His life seemed to be in less danger; his humiliation did not diminish: constant, harassing work, total solitude. His only consolation came from Christ Himself.

Winter came and went, without a ray of hope. Gradually the most savage of the Indians grew accustomed to seeing the white slave living among them. They listened to him speak from his vast store of knowledge — of the moon, the stars, the seasons, the mysteries of the world. He was allowed to move about freely, to go from wigwam to wigwam. This gave him the opportunity to baptize some children, some of the sick, and even a few adult Indians. One of his former torturers, a man who had torn off two of his fingernails, was so touched by the way the missionary had cared for him during an illness that he took Fr. Jogues under his protection. Better yet, he was allowed to send word to other missionaries who had thought him dead, and even an urgent letter to the French governor, explaining how an expedition might be organized, what means to employ, and what perils to avoid. He had no thought of rescue for himself. He would remain a slave among his persecutors so that he could speak to them of Christ as long as possible and help his fellow prisoners, the Hurons, many of them Christians themselves. This strange, sublime life lasted a year.

On July 31, 1643, a year to the day after the convoy had left Trois-Rivières on its ill-fated return voyage, Providence offered the missionary another chance. The Mohawks had journeyed to a Dutch trading post on the banks of the Hudson to transact a barter deal. To show the whites their own power, they brought along their white slave. A Protestant pastor attached to the post befriended Fr. Jogues and invited him to be his guest. When the pastor proposed to help him escape, however, the Jesuit refused. He had just learned that the Mohawks were finally going to make good their threat to burn their Huron prisoners alive. He must remain with them to bring them supreme succor.

At the moment of his decision, the Indians were thrown into tumult by the news that the French had attacked the Iroquois at two points and had routed a large force of Indian warriors. The hate of the Indians focused upon the missionary. The white slave's letter had brought on this disaster. Vengeance was impossible as long as his captors were camped near the Dutch trading post, but as soon as they moved on, he was sure to be killed. What should he do?

Night after night, the Jesuit prayed for guidance. He was thirty-seven years old; he might have many more years ahead of him to live and work for God. Should he deliberately court certain death? His escape would no longer harm very many. Most of his fellow captives were now either dead or had escaped. It seemed to him that God would want him to flee.

Anchored in the broad Hudson was a ship about to sail for Europe. Fr. Jogues had spoken to the captain, who had given his word as a sailor that he would take the Frenchman back to France. All that was needed was a small craft and darkness, but it was not as simple as it seemed.

On his first attempt, barking dogs aroused the Mohawk sentries before Fr. Jogues could reach his canoe. On the second try, his canoe stuck fast on a sandbar. The missionary was not strong enough to push it free. He was just about to give up when a surge of the current floated it off. He paddled to the ship's side and clambered aboard. He was safe at last!

But it was not to be. His escape was discovered before the ship sailed. The Mohawk chiefs went to the Dutch. If the ship sailed with their slave, they would kill every Hollander at the post and burn the buildings to the ground.

When Fr. Jogues heard of this ultimatum, he forbade the captain to weigh anchor. No one else should suffer on his account. He returned to shore and what he believed would be his end. Even if the Hollanders refused to give him up to the Indians, he was going to die. He was sick at heart and of body. The cruel wounds made by his Indian torturers had never quite healed. He feared that gangrene was about to set in in one leg.

But while the Bears and Wolves of the Iroquois were again haggling over the question of burning their fugitive slave alive as soon as he was returned, Providence once more intervened on behalf of the future saint. Orders came from the Netherlands to save the French missionary. Anne of Austria, Queen of France, had heard of the desperate plight of the heroic Jesuit and had asked the Dutch Crown to organize his rescue.

September: The port of New Amsterdam on Manhattan Island. The waterfront was crowded with onlookers to watch the Jesuit go aboard his ship. Jogues would have never believed that he would be so famous.

November: The Atlantic had not been kind to the miserable little vermin-infested ship that was taking the missionary home. For two months, the little craft was buffeted by storms, blown off its course, and close to foundering several times. The crew, all Protestants, blamed the near-catastrophic passage on the fact that there was a Catholic priest aboard. When the ship limped into Falmouth with its lateen sail and its jib, its only canvas, in tatters, the crew rushed ashore. Left behind alone, Fr. Jogues was nearly killed by wharf rats who came aboard to plunder the ship. A shot fired at him barely missed. It was weeks before he could get passage to France.

On Christmas Eve 1643, the parish priest at Saint-Pol-de-Léon, a fishing port on the Channel coast of Britanny, was preparing to celebrate the three Low Masses when a man in rags entered his chapel and knelt before him, begging to have his confession heard so that he might receive Holy Communion. When he said that he was Fr. Jogues and had just come back from Canada, the priest was stunned. All France knew in a general way how many missionaries had been martyred overseas.

A rich merchant of the port took the missionary to Rennes, where he humbly knocked at the door of the Jesuit college there without identifying himself.

"So you've just come from New France?" said the Father Superior. "Then you must know some of our Jesuit fathers over there."

"Very well indeed, Father."

"How is Fr. de Brébeuf getting along?"

"He is in very good health."

"And Fr. Jogues, who was captured by the Indians and went through such frightful torture — is he still alive?"

"He is indeed, Father. I am Fr. Jogues."

Sudden glory descended upon the missionary. The contemporary newspapers detailed his adventures, his suffering, and his heroism. To escape from the curious, he took refuge in Clermont College (today Lycée Louis-le-Grand) in Paris. Queen Anne received him, surrounded by her two sons, Louis XIV and Philippe, and her whole court of princes and princesses. Cardinal Mazarin summoned him to report on the situation in New France. The queen summed up the unanimous opinion of the country when she declared, "Every day we read adventure novels that are pure fiction. Here we have one that is true, and which blends the heroic with the miraculous." And when the Pope was asked to give special dispensation to Fr. Jogues so that he might celebrate the Mass in his own way, since his mutilated hands would not permit him to perform all the liturgical gestures, Urban VIII exclaimed, "It would be indeed unjust to refuse the blood of Christ to a martyr of Christ."

However, in the midst of all this glory, Fr. Jogues was disturbed. He could not help thinking constantly of Canada, of his Christian Hurons, of his friends who must have been discouraged by his departure. He went to see his superiors and begged leave to return. It was granted. At the end of April 1644, he set sail from La Rochelle. It was not to be his fate to live out his days peacefully in France. As an Adventurer of God, he must return to the fight.

He found the situation in Canada as bad as ever. The Indians were still at war with one another. Massacres were still the order of the day. Iroquois were doing their best to annihilate Hurons and Algonquins. An Italian Jesuit father had just been tortured. Fr. Jogues asked for a post in the most difficult and dangerous region on the edge of Mohawk country.

Once installed, he immediately resumed contact with the Mohawks. He knew many of them and planned to use his knowledge of the Wolf Tribe to re-establish peace. He called a conference between the Iroquois and the French, and later hundreds of pirogues arrived carrying the braves of three peoples, all wearing white paint, the color of peace. The talks went on for months. The exchange of prisoners was arranged.

Ambassadors were to be reinstated from people to people. The war hatchet was buried. Peace appeared to be established. The great adventure seemed finished.

But not for Fr. Jogues. Since ambassadors were to be sent to the Five Nations of the Iroquois, he would be one of them. He would be emissary to the most savage of them, his old torturers, the Mohawks. While waiting for his request to be approved by his superiors, he went into a most rigid retreat, as though he knew that his martyrdom was near. In the spring, he left for his new post, buoyed by supernatural joy. "A mission to the Iroquois," he wrote, "seemed to me the fulfillment of my dreams."

When he reached his destination after a long and difficult journey, the Mohawks greeted his return with astonishment, amazed by the courage of the paleface. The old woman who had once protected him gave her "nephew" the fondest of welcomes. The way seemed smoother now. In the future, missionaries would be able to sow the seed of the Gospel with full hands. After several peaceful months of friendly talk, Fr. Jogues returned to headquarters to report on his mission. Peace had been re-established. An apostolate would henceforth be possible. He was an optimist.

One morning in late September 1646, a heavy fog veiled the St. Lawrence River at Trois-Rivières. Fr. Jogues had said Mass at the Residency of the Jesuit Fathers and made his way to the riverbank, where the pirogues were loaded and waiting. He bade his brothers goodbye and pushed off for the upstream journey to Mohawk country.

After the first day's journey, the missionary was aware of a vague feeling of menace that hung over the expedition. The feeling increased steadily, grew more tangible. Without warning, his Iroquois escorts disappeared overnight. The Huron ambassadors, after several mysterious meetings, pulled out of the convoy to go home. The Jesuit missionary was alone with his French companion, Jean de la Lande, and one faithful Indian guide.

The three men left the St. Lawrence to paddle up the Richelieu River. They traveled south, carrying their canoe around the rapids, into Lake Champlain. As they stepped ashore, Fr. Jogues noted a file of Indians drawn up some distance away. He called to them, raised his arms in greeting. The reply was ominous silence. None of them moved.

Perhaps they did not recognize their old friend Ondessonk. He walked closer, then stopped. His heart sank. The Mohawks were again smeared with red war paint. They were armed to the teeth. The buried hatchet had been dug up.

With wild war whoops, the Indians bore down on the missionary and his two friends, beat them to the ground, bound them hand and foot. The old story began again: captivity, fatigue, beatings, suffering. The Mohawks did not yet dare torture him, but that, too, would come. Was he not responsible for the epidemic and the long dry spell that had plagued the Mohawks in his absence? The radical Bear faction thought so. The evil spells cast by the white man had brought them misfortune. The palefaces must be sacrificed to the manitous. The war must be resumed.

The men of the Wolves dissented. Why not let well enough alone? Why anger the whites as well as the manitous? The argument went on for days. "Which was worse: displeasing the whites or irritating the manitous? The Wolves proposed holding the Frenchmen as hostages; the Bears would sacrifice them at once. Overhearing the arguments, Fr. Jogues prepared himself for death.

One evening a Bear invited the missionary to his wigwam for supper. His friends advised him against it. They tried to detain him, but Fr. Jogues would not listen. When he started off in silence, his old "aunt" went with him. He followed his host through a cold, dismal mist that filled the dusk. At the entrance to a wigwam, the Indian made signs for the Jesuit to enter. The missionary raised the flap of skins that served as a door. In the shadow he saw a man standing with one arm upraised, a tomahawk in his hand.

The arm flashed down. The tomahawk crashed against the nape of Fr. Jogues's neck. A second blow crushed his skull. His body was dragged from the wigwam. A crowd gathered while he was being scalped. Then he was decapitated, and his head, impaled on a stake, was carried through the village like a trophy of war. The Indians howled with delirious joy.

St. Isaac Jogues had met the end that his heart desired. He had shed his blood for Christ.

Bl. Junípero Serra

∽

Creator of California

Among the points of interest sought out by visitors to the Capitol at Washington, D.C., is the National Hall of Statuary. Situated in the old hall of the House of Representatives, Statuary Hall was created by an act of Congress in 1864 and contains forty-eight bronze statues set upon marble pedestals, each inscribed in gold letters with the name of a man and the name of a state. Each state was originally invited to contribute not more than two statues of men considered worthy of national commemoration, but in 1933, the number in Statuary Hall was limited to one for each state, with the rest placed in the Rotunda and elsewhere in the Capitol.

One of the forty-eight statues stands out because of its unusual attire. Among the frock coats of the statesmen, the military uniforms of the generals, and the fur hats of the pioneers, there is a tonsured little man in a long robe, his bare feet in sandals, one hand holding the model of a church, the other raising a large cross. He is easily recognizable as a Franciscan. The name of the state engraved beneath his statue: California.

Heroes of God

If we look at the map of California, we cannot help being struck by the considerable number of cities and towns bearing the names of saints, particularly saints connected with the Franciscan Order. San Francisco, for instance, honors the founder himself, the gentle and generous Poverello of Assisi. Some fifty miles to the south, in a smiling valley of orchards and vineyards, we find Santa Clara, named for the great friend and collaborator of St. Francis, St. Clare, founder of the Clarist Sisters. St. Anthony of Padua, the great Franciscan preacher of southern France, has given his name to a river in central California and a hamlet on the edge of the Mojave Desert: San Antonio. And San Juan Capistrano, with its lovely mission gardens and its homing swallows, bears the name of another illustrious Franciscan preacher, St. John Capistran, whose eloquence moved thousands in Bohemia and Moravia and who led the Crusaders against the Turks besieging Belgrade in the fifteenth century.

Even the glamour city of the state, the motion-picture capital of the world (since Hollywood is actually only a district within its municipality), Los Angeles, bears the name in the Franciscan tradition. The original Spanish name for Los Angeles was *El Pueblo de Nuestra Señora de los Angeles*, and the Franciscan Order was founded in the Church of Our Lady of the Angels.

The modest Franciscan who has been immortalized in bronze in the Capitol of the American nation has thus left his mark on the state that chose him as one of the two most distinguished Californians. And what a mark! Today hundreds of thousands of tourists travel over his Camino Real every year to visit the places where he lived, and the museums dedicated to his memory, inspecting such relics as the packsaddles of his mules and the caldrons in which he cooked the food for his beloved Indians. California schoolchildren learn his name as soon as they begin to read, the name inscribed on the pedestal at the Capitol in Washington: Junípero Serra.

Junípero Serra: The family name is Spanish, or more exactly, Majorcan, for like Bl. Ramon Lull, the first missionary to Africa, the future missionary to California was born in Majorca, in the Balearics, the son of a poor quarry worker, in 1713. As for his given name, all who have read the *Fioretti* of St. Francis[19] must recognize its origin; they would remember the good Br. Juniper who pretended to be mad so that he might suffer humiliations similar to those inflicted upon the Savior.

Ever since Ramon Lull, a Franciscan himself, the sons of St. Francis have been both numerous and powerful in Majorca. Bl. Ramon himself founded the University of Palma, which in his lifetime was one of the best of the kingdom. When he entered the Order of the Gray Brothers and donned their sandals and their rough drugget robe, little Miguel Serra (who later adopted the religious name of Junípero) was not long in attracting attention as a young man of great promise. His appearance, it must be said, was not in his favor. He was far from

---

[19] *The Little Flowers of Francis of Assisi*, a classic collection of popular legends about the life of St. Francis of Assisi and his companions.

prepossessing — a thin, undersized youth with sickly features. And yet to anyone who spoke to him, he radiated uncommon intelligence and strength that quickly created a surprising impression on his betters.

As soon as he had finished his seven-year course of studies in philosophy and theology at the University of Palma, he was appointed to the faculty. For ten years, he taught the erudite subjects that he had learned so well.

But it was not to become a professor that the little Junípero had become a monk. He had read books of his illustrious compatriot, Bl. Ramon, who set forth most lucidly the reasons why it was a Christian duty to carry the Word to peoples who were still pagan. He had read the passionate and pathetic stories of the great Spanish missionaries who followed in the footsteps of the conquistadors to plant the cross in the immense spaces of Mexico and South America. His favorite was the delightful St. Francis Solano, who, at the end of the sixteenth century, traveled through Peru, Chile, and much of what is now Argentina, playing the violin to win over the most savage peoples, and who alone baptized no fewer than one hundred thousand Indians.

In 1748, when he was thirty-five, Junípero Serra heard that the Franciscan fathers of Mexico were seeking volunteers for their missions. Their celebrated San Fernando College, veritable headquarters for the evangelization of the Indians, needed thirty-three Adventurers of God. The young professor of the University of Palma offered his services. It was not a simple matter to be accepted. His academic and religious superiors were reluctant to release so able a professor. Fra Junípero not only had to pull many strings, but he even had to resort to tricks (albeit holy tricks) to gain his ends. He finally succeeded. When some of the missionary recruits caught first sight of the cockleshell of a boat in which they were expected to cross the ocean, they withdrew. Replacements had to be quickly found. Fra Junípero just happened to be handy.

Sailing on a mission to the New World was still a great adventure in mid-eighteenth century. From Palma to Mexico was a voyage of at least eighteen months — a year and a half aboard a tiny, crowded ship, dangerous in stormy weather, most uncomfortable in calm seas; a year and a half on foul, scanty rations, and on such short freshwater rations that a glass of water a day was considered generous. Once ashore, the missionaries were not much better off. The difficult roads were under constant menace of attack by hostile Indians. The risks of disease and climate and the threat of venomous snakes and insects were ever present.

Fra Junípero Serra's first contact with North American soil taught him much. On the road from Vera Cruz to Mexico City, he was stung in the leg by a scorpion. The poison produced frightful sores that never healed properly and, although he had escaped death, left him with a limp for the rest of his life. A painful beginning!

∞

The heroes of God seem to have thrived on obstacles and personal peril, and eighteenth-century Mexico lacked neither. The Spanish had garrisoned the principal cities and had established their military outposts — *presidios* — in widespread points throughout the country. The missionaries followed the flag pretty closely and established their evangelical centers in the wake of the military. But the roads were risky, and it was not safe to venture far from the larger garrisons without armed escort. Many an unprotected convoy was ambushed, plundered, and massacred by the Indians. Volleys of poisoned arrows flew whistling from the underbrush without warning. Shots rang out — from firearms stolen from the Spaniards. Whole groups of travelers disappeared without a trace.

Among the fiercest of the aboriginal tribes, the Pame Indians of the Sierra Gorda ranked high. They were cannibals, for one thing, who ate human flesh only when cooked with tomatoes and chili peppers — a sauce, incidentally, still popular in Mexico although now containing less sinister ingredients. An official report admitted that all military expeditions attempting to penetrate the thick jungles sheltering the Pames were unsuccessful, and that missionary efforts to convert these Indians had failed. And yet it was necessary to do something about a menace that had become so bold that raiding parties frequently ventured from the region of Jalpan to strike at the much-traveled highway from Querétaro to Mexico City.

Soon after his arrival in San Fernando, Fra Junípero learned that another attempt was to be made to baptize the Pames of the Sierra Gorda. He volunteered enthusiastically. What finer dream than to die a martyr! His reputation for intelligence, firmness of character, and saintliness was already so great within his order that his superiors at San Fernando named him prefect of the little company of ten brothers who were going to attempt the Sierra Gorda venture. In all humility, Fra Junípero protested against the title — in vain. Prefect he was, and prefect he would remain.

Fra Junípero remained in Pame country for eight years. Amazingly enough, he was not devoured by the Indians. He was not even attacked. From the first, he employed a method that became increasingly effective. He remembered that the missionaries of the Middle Ages had taught the techniques of material civilization at the same time they were teaching the spiritual values of Christianity. As soon as Fra Junípero had settled his little group of brothers in the Pame country, he set about teaching the Indians how to cut down trees, plow the ground, plant corn, and breed cattle, sheep, and mules. The happy results of his efforts gradually became known throughout the Sierra Gorda. Not only the Pames, but also other tribes discovered that the methods taught by the white missionaries led to a better and easier life than that to be had by depending entirely on the hunt and the products of the forest. The new missionary centers that sprang up were also centers for agriculture and stock-raising.

The Spanish military leaders were dumbfounded by the success of unarmed monks in the same area that had fiercely defied Spanish muskets and cavalry sabers. Junípero and his brothers, however, did not permit their material progress to divert them from their evangelical goal. They worked hard at converting their Pames to Christianity. They translated the catechism into Pame, preached in Pame, and heard confessions in Pame. They discredited the witch doctors. The old idols of the Sun Mother were overthrown, some burned, others ceremoniously presented to the missionaries.

Heroes of God

The good Franciscan fathers found themselves running a little communal republic in which the converted Indians worked together, shared the products of their common cultivation of the soil, and prayed together. It was a triumph. The impenetrable Sierra Gorda had become God's province.

The spectacular success of the lame little brother influenced both his religious superiors and the Spanish lay authorities to utilize his remarkable talents as a pacifier in a field still more difficult than that of the Pames. They would send him to the Apaches. What was then known as "Apache country" was situated roughly in what is now the states of Texas, New Mexico, and Arizona. Actually, Apache country constituted a vast and ill-defined region also inhabited by Indian tribes other than the Apaches who had little in common except their ferocity. The Apaches were reputed to be cannibals without the epicurean finesse of the Pames. Instead of stewing their prisoners in a pot with tomatoes and chili peppers, they merely flayed them alive, bled them well (they were not fond of red meat), and roasted them on a spit. The transference of the name of "Apaches" to the worst bandits of the Paris underworld seems to have had some justification.

When Junípero Serra arrived in this dreadful Apache country, the Indians had just killed two missionaries under the most frightful circumstances. This did not prevent his attempting to evangelize them — in vain. The malice of some men can defeat even the charity, the zeal, and the heroism of saints. Other missionaries were murdered by these intractable savages, whose trickery was as dangerous as their violence. One Apache tribe would come knocking at the gates of a Spanish *presidio*, asking protection against an enemy tribe. No sooner had they been admitted to the stockade than the Indians produced tomahawks, quivers of arrows, and muskets stolen from the French in Louisiana — and the massacre began. After several tragedies of this sort and the failure of attempts to convert the Apaches, the mission superiors recalled Junípero and his group.

For several years, Fra Junípero devoted himself to preaching. He visited the missions in numerous cities, towns, and villages of the dioceses of Mexico, Puebla, Morelos, and Oaxaca, speaking constantly of Christ, of His Passion, and of His love for mankind. His warm, simple eloquence won many hearts. Sometimes, to demonstrate to his listeners the necessity of penance, he would bare his breast and shoulders and castigate himself with such violence that his skin was beaded with blood. And yet this fiery little man who seemed so terrible in the pulpit appeared to those who came to him for advice as the gentlest, most delicate, and most understanding of soul counselors. And the fame that he acquired as missionary to the Sierra Gorda continued to grow.

Then in 1767, an unexpected event launched him in a new direction. As a result of a hundred complicated incidents and innumerable intrigues, the Spanish government exiled the Jesuits from both Spain and the colonies, a rather singular measure when we consider the great part played by the fathers of the Society of Jesus in evangelizing the world, particularly Spanish America. The political considerations behind the anti-Jesuit action make a long and involved story that we need not go into here. Suffice it to say that the 178 Jesuits living in Mexico were expelled by order of the viceroy. Rather than abandon the many missions they had founded, the Jesuits appealed to other orders to take them over, notably the Franciscans.

Among these missions were fifteen the Jesuits had established on the long narrow peninsula that paralleled the Pacific Coast of Mexico for some eight hundred miles. Many of the stations bore the names of Jesuit saints: San Ignacio, San Francisco Javier, San Francisco de Borja. It was Junípero Serra who was chosen to take over for the exiled missionaries.

"Lower California," as it was to be called, to distinguish the peninsula from the continental California that was to become an American state, was a pretty wild country in the eighteenth century. The Indians were not very civilized, and the Spanish soldiers in the rare *presidios* were on a constant alert. Fra Junípero, however, was used to this sort of thing. As soon as he arrived, he began the same system that had worked so well with the Pames. He taught the natives agriculture and cattle-raising, how to organize their villages and to live like white men. After a year of considerable progress, Fra Junípero and his companions were assigned to a much more daring project.

∞

North of the Lower California peninsula was a vast mountainous region that had stopped the boldest of Spanish explorers at its shores. Some thirty maritime expeditions had probed its coastline, but none had investigated the interior, none had thought of starting a settlement, and few had put landing parties ashore. They had mapped several anchorages, San Diego,

Santa Barbara, and Monterey, although what previous navigators called "San Francisco Bay" was an unsheltered cove some twenty miles to the north, today called Drake's Bay; the great harbor of San Francisco was not to be discovered for another year or so. The coastal range of mountains, the early explorers assumed, dipped again to the sea on the far side — apparently an extension of the Gulf of California, they said. As for the people of the country, little was known except that they were Indians, very likely Apaches, and that they went around naked because the climate was so delightful.

Why did Madrid suddenly order an expedition to push into this unknown land? For a very curious reason that will be well understood by Americans today. The chancelleries of Europe were agog with the rumor that the czarina of Russia — none other than the notorious Catherine II, whose personal and territorial ambitions were considerable — was about to extend her expansionist program to the New World. A Russian expedition would cross the Pacific to occupy the western coast of North America in the name of the czarina. A Russian colony on the borders of the Spanish lands in America would indeed constitute a danger to peace and to Spanish prestige, so the Viceroy of Mexico took matters into his own hands and decided to build a fortress at Monterey capable of repelling a Russian invasion of California.

Remembering the fine work that Fra Junípero had done in the Sierra Gorda, the viceroy summoned the missionary to Mexico City and asked him to accompany the military expedition, using his now-famous Pame methods to pacify the California Indians by founding missions along the supply line. A missionary to the depths of his soul, Junípero Serra accepted with joy.

This was in 1768. For the next sixteen years, until the day of his death, the little monk with the limp would be the director of this astonishing project: to rescue for civilization this wild new country, to plant the Cross along some six hundred miles of coastline. His poor leg still pained him. The ulceration refused to heal, and his limp was more and more pronounced. Other maladies were to be added to his physical handicap: chronic bronchitis and frequent serious attacks of gastritis. And the life he was forced to lead was hardly designed for a semi-invalid.

Picture the makeup of an expedition heading into this unknown country. A troop of some twenty mounted cuirassiers; a company of sappers to clear the trail, cut down trees, and improvise bridges; Indian archers recruited from Christianized tribes; a whole little world of laborers, cooks, farmers, and herdsmen; not to mention the mass of bleating, bellowing animals who were brought along for the double purpose of furnishing food during the journey and of forming the nuclei of farming colonies once settlements were established.

The expedition was in constant danger. Valleys and mountain passes were all potential points of ambush. The camps were heavily guarded at night. Despite this, there were several bloody attacks by Indians. But the column pushed on to found a series of combination missions and military outposts along a coast that today is one of the world's favorite recreation areas. And the present names of the missions designate pleasant beaches, stylish resorts, and restful vacation spots.

As soon as one mission was founded — they were situated one day's march apart — Fra Junípero put his system into operation. Love and gentleness were his secret ingredients. How he cherished his Indians! He spoke warmly of their natural virtues, the rare qualities they possessed, which needed only Baptism to come into full flower. He found no fault with them, which is saying much. According to him, they had only to hear of the beauties of the holy Christian religion to become converted, to become better, more civilized men than many Europeans. He suffered agonies whenever events proved him wrong; when, for example, a few renegade Christian Indians would attack a mission. He suffered even more when European soldiers, who were far from all being saints, used violence on the Indians or launched reprisals. The most surprising thing was that, on the whole, Fra Junípero's methods were quite successful.

Soon each of his mission stations became a true center of European civilization. The three or four Franciscan fathers who maintained each mission taught the Indians the cultivation of soil, the raising of livestock, and even a few rural crafts. Numerically, the project really didn't amount to very much at the start: only a few hundred Indians were ready to come and live under the protection of the white men and listen to their counsel. Beyond the missions many dangers still existed, and communications between stations could be maintained only under heavy escort. Furthermore, the methods of kindness often seemed pretty absurd to the Spanish soldiers charged with pacifying the country. They believed that only force could maintain law and order. A good massacre from time to time would keep the Indians in line.

Junípero Serra naturally opposed the military viewpoint, and he went so far as to protest the policy of force to Don Antonio María Bucareli y Ursúa, the Viceroy, Governor, and Captain General of New Spain. Fortunately the viceroy was a true Christian who understood the great missionary's viewpoint. Yet, despite the backing of Mexico City, of the sixteen years he devoted to the creation of California, Fra Junípero spent no fewer than six or seven of them in fighting the stupidity of lay administrators and military officers who thought only in terms of killing. Some of them were so disgusted with the Franciscan's methods and influence that they recommended to Mexico City that the whole California project be abandoned.

Abandon California? Again Fra Junípero was up in arms. The little monk fought this new proposition with such fierce energy that once more it was to him that Mexico City listened. Even if the danger of a Russian invasion seemed to have passed, there could be no question of leaving a Christian work half done. As long as he lived, Junípero Serra would not desert his cherished Indians who had put their trust in him, who had asked to be baptized. No, the work must be carried forward as far as possible.

It was a great joy for the tireless founder, who had always believed that Upper California would one day become a Christian land, to learn in 1776 that his old friend and spiritual brother, one of his valued collaborators, Fr. Francisco Palou, had taken a little group of priests north of Monterey and founded a new mission that would bear the most illustrious name in all the great Franciscan family: San Francisco.

Creator of California

To judge the results of all this admirable enterprise, of all this effort expended with such risk and trouble, we must jump twenty years ahead to the beginning of the nineteenth century. By that time, the whole coast, from San Diego to San Francisco, had been occupied and pacified. From the shores of the Pacific to the edge of the desert, all the Indians had become Christians. The missions had continued to multiply: Santa Barbara, La Puríssima Concepción, San Miguel, Solano, San José, San Francisco — and many others. There was no longer any need of mounted cuirassiers with their muskets to maintain law and order. To found a new mission, all that was needed was to send two Franciscan fathers with an escort of four or five men. The Indians had learned the advantages of European civilization and were eager for education.

The land had been transformed. From the moment the first white men saw the country, they had noted that north of the thirtieth parallel, the climate was really ideal, that the valleys were carpeted with vigorous green grass, and that the hillsides were covered with wild grapevines. Fra Junípero Serra had sent to Europe for seeds and plants, and in accordance with his wishes, the Indians quickly learned to grow fruits and vegetables. Acres and acres were gradually given over to olive trees, orange groves, vineyards, and fruit trees of all kinds. They flourished, better than in Spain, even better than in Andalucía. The local-born horses turned out to be an excellent breed, hardy and lively.

And even better, California was getting roads, real roads with solid bridges. There were even canals. There were also mills and workshops for all trades. California was becoming self-sufficient. A visiting traveler exclaimed, "This is the Spanish Arcadia!" And another traveler, a Protestant, declared, "I have never seen a happier people than those who live in this land." George Vancouver, the British navigator who sailed with Cook and later explored the American Pacific coast on his own, wrote his own explanation of the apparent miracle: "To what should we attribute this unheard-of opulence if not to the strict husbandry and to the sacrifices which the monks endured from the start?" This is true. Without Junípero Serra and his team of Franciscans, California would not have been the same.

At the threshold of the nineteenth century, this Franciscan California was a veritable republic of happiness. The father-directors governed a commonwealth divided into twenty-odd missions, each composed of two thousand natives. It might have been called an immense monastery, for the society was ruled by Christian principles. The Gospel was law. Private property did not exist. All property and goods belonged to the community, and the father divided it according to the needs of each family, so that all should be well provided for. Daily life was attuned to the rhythm of prayer, Divine Office, and religious ceremonies, a routine that nobody dreamed of avoiding. It seemed like Paradise on earth.

But this marvelous experiment was not to last. In 1821, Mexico, having declared its independence from the Spanish Crown, attacked and captured California. Twelve years later, during a series of violent crises that gripped the state all through the nineteenth century, an anticlerical government decreed that all missions must be secularized. The Franciscans were expelled from the land they had created. It was not until 1847, fourteen years after their exile, that the United States, having defeated Mexico by force of arms, acquired the vast territory that comprises today Texas, New Mexico, and Upper California, could resume the work of civilization.

By that time, the great missionary who had laid the foundations for California had been dead for more than sixty years. In 1784, Fra Junípero Serra died the holiest of deaths. He had insisted that he be stretched out upon the ground in token of his humility, invoking with his last breath the Lord Jesus and the Virgin Mary. His brothers who entered his poor cell found him on the ground, asleep in God. He was clasping to his breast the great crucifix from which, day and night, even in sleep, he was never separated.

Bl. Anne-Marie Javouhey

∽

Apostle of Racial Charity

On his way to Paris to place the imperial crown upon the head
of Napoleon Bonaparte, Pope Pius VII stopped at Chalon-sur-
Saône to celebrate Easter. The year was 1804. All of Burgundy
rushed to Chalon to acclaim the Supreme Pontiff, whose warm
smile and luminous eyes touched every heart. In the crowd
were four peasant girls, all sisters, who had come from their
village of Chamblanc, southeast of Dijon, to kneel before the
Holy Father. Their trip was inspired largely by curiosity, albeit
a pious curiosity. They attended the Pope's Mass and received
Communion from his hands. Then they waited, their young
hearts full of hope. The four girls had had the audacity to ask
for a private audience. They hoped that the priest who had offered to act as intermediary would be as persuasive and eloquent
as they had been bold. By a miracle, he was. He told the illustrious traveler that the girls were good Christians and engaged
in village charities, so His Holiness granted them an audience.

The Holy Father asked them questions, encouraged them
in their works, and blessed them with the kindness that

marked everything he did, whether concerned with the smallest details of everyday life or the great upheavals of history. The girls went home by the road that followed the River Saône, now certain that God was satisfied with their work.

They were the four daughters of Master Balthazar Javouhey, a solid Burgundian peasant, well established on fertile land, who was a good Christian and also, like most Burgundians, a good epicurean. His eldest daughter, the one who had led the quartet to Chalon, was a healthy, rosy-cheeked girl, as merry as a warbler, who impressed everyone by her intelligence and courage. At her baptism, she was given the name Anne Marie, but everyone who knew her — and most of the countryside did — called her Nanette. The three other youngsters — the calm and cautious Pierette; the meek Marie Françoise, who was afraid of everything; and the quick, sprightly, roguish Claudine, the youngest — all swore by Nanette and would obey few other than their big sister. There was no adventure they would not undertake if she gave the word. And it was indeed an adventure on which she was leading them.

A fiery maiden was this Nanette. She served God with a passion that would admit of no old-maidish bigotry or chicken-hearted timidity. Born in 1779, she was still a little girl during the black years of the French Revolution, yet she was without peer in the art of hiding priests from their tormentors or of helping them escape from the sans-culottes. She had been seen helping an old curé across the Saône and was known to have organized clandestine Masses for courageous Christians. More than once the revolutionaries suspected that their clerical game was getting away, thanks to this sly little gamin, but they dared not arrest a child of thirteen. One day when a Revolutionary mob invaded the Chamblanc château and set fire to it, a girlish figure was seen silhouetted against the flames, running for dear life, clasping to her bosom the monstrance and the holy vessels she had rescued from the blazing chapel. It was of course the little Javouhey girl.

It was inevitable that a girl of such a nature should choose an unusual life for herself. Not the life, perhaps, that her father had in mind when he introduced her to a nice, decent local boy who would certainly make her a good husband and who would help her manage a few of the family farms. However, she spoke so eloquently to her suitor of the love of God and the religious life, that instead of marrying her, he became a Trappist monk. As for Nanette herself, she had long since made up her own mind. She was still a small child, praying devoutly as she did so often at the village church, when she seemed to hear an inner voice saying to her, "Thou wilt belong to me. Thou wilt be consecrated to me. Thou wilt serve the poor and care for the orphans."

She was nineteen when she and her three sisters decided to devote themselves entirely to teaching the catechism to the village children and to helping the needy. These were solemn vows, solemnly taken in a room of the farmhouse made into an improvised chapel. And her father was deeply disturbed.

Nanette a nun? What a waste, declared Master Balthazar. Nanette was a better man than either of his two sons! She was the one who should manage the family estates, instead of telling her beads all day. What was worse, since she had this bee in her bonnet, she was quite capable of talking her two brothers into taking the vows (which, incidentally, is exactly what happened!). But Nanette resisted all argument and all pressure with calm kindness and a disarming smile. A nun she wanted to be; a nun she would be.

Actually, finding the right path that would lead her to God was not easy. It took many years of groping before she could formulate for herself a task that would fill a real void. At first, we saw her installed in a country house, continuing her work of charity and of teaching the catechism to the village children. For a while, she thought of entering a convent and leading a cloistered life — a surprising idea for such an active and passionate soul. For another period, she worked in the Jura mountains near the Swiss border, trying against long financial odds to create small peasant communities at Souvans, or near Dôle. The vocation that drove her was so powerfully original that it is not surprising that it took so long for her to break out of her chrysalis. Once she had spread her wings, however, the butterfly would fly far.

Interviews with a saintly priest, the enlightened counsel of a great monk, Dom de Lestrange of the Trappist Abbey of Val-Sainte in Switzerland, and profound meditations during which the light of Christ often shone in her soul all convinced her that, although the road was rough and winding, it was nevertheless leading her to her true goal. The village priest of Chamblanc, returning to his parish after the stormy revolutionary years, marveled at the good that the Javouhey girls had done. He decided at once that Anne Marie was an exceptional person destined for great things, but he was mistaken in recommending to her father that she enter an established congregation. At the convent of the Sisters of Charity in Besançon, while she meditated profoundly and prayed to God for enlightenment on which road to follow, she had a vision. Just as St. Francis Xavier, at the moment of his definitive choice, saw himself carrying an Ethiopian slave on his back, so did Anne Marie, to her great stupefaction, see herself surrounded by men with black skin, holding out their arms to her.

Now, rural education of this period was not very thorough in France, and a country girl like Anne Marie had never learned that there were such people as Negroes among God's creatures. But before she had recovered from her amazement, she heard a voice saying firmly, "These are the children God is giving you. I am St. Teresa,[20] and I will be the patron saint of your order."

The missionary vocation of Anne Marie Javouhey was born.

∞

After years of hesitation and groping, everything suddenly seemed very simple to Anne Marie. She explained her grand design to Monsignor de Fontanges, Bishop of Chalon, who understood, approved, and gave the four Javouhey sisters the wing of an old Benedictine convent for their work, which, for the time being, would continue to be chiefly the Christian education of little girls. In the meantime, Anne Marie had persuaded her brother Pierre to recruit volunteers for a parallel project for boys. In 1807, three years after Pope Pius VII had

---

[20] St. Teresa of Avila (1515-1582), Carmelite nun and mystic.

blessed the four peasant girls, they founded the Religious Society of St. Joseph. On May 12, at the Church of St. Peter, they pronounced their final vows and took the habit of the new congregation. The blue of their robes, blue as a May sky, was the same blue worn by the girl grape-pickers of Burgundy. The big hood fell to their shoulders, and the plastron was wide and white. The new society was activated.

Soon the new group was moved to Cluny, near Mâcon, where better quarters were available, and the nuns became popularly known as the Sisters of St. Joseph of Cluny.

To make good Christians of the children of France was certainly one of the principal aims of Mother Javouhey, but it was not the only one. Cluny, the headquarters and novitiate of the congregation, was a flourishing school for the middle classes. In the Marais quarter of Paris, the Sisters of St. Joseph opened an experimental school to try out the newest methods of pedagogy. But these were merely stepping-stones to the real goal of the founder: to teach black children Christianity, and to build hospitals for the treatment of black patients. Educator, missionary, and sister of charity: these were her aims with regard to her congregation as viewed by Anne Marie Javouhey. After all, there were many media for bringing the message of Christ to the world.

The opportunity finally came, as it always does to those whom Providence has designated. Recently arrived in Paris was the Governor of Bourbon Island — now Réunion — who briefed the French Government on current conditions in the island, materially prosperous, but morally bankrupt. The natives were wallowing in ignorance and the worst sort of negligence. "I have just what you need," said Viscount Laîné, Minister of the Interior. Mother Javouhey was summoned and listened without surprise — after all, was not God with her? — to a proposition to give her control of the charitable works and the education of the island. She accepted at once. A few months later, four sisters in the blue robes of St. Joseph sailed for a long voyage to the Indian Ocean. The first stone of a great missionary structure had just been laid.

Mother Javouhey did not go herself. Not that she did not want to sail. But she felt it was too soon to leave her work in France. Besides, she had another project in mind. Had not her vision told her that it was in Africa, the Dark Continent, that her true mission lay? It was in Africa that she was to plant the Cross.

France at this time did not possess the vast empire from the Congo to the Mediterranean that she achieved in the nineteenth and twentieth centuries, but she had one port of entry to Black Africa: Senegal. It was not much, unfortunately. A badly administered colony under the influence of the shadiest traders; a black population that had learned nothing from the French except their bad habits; a shabby capital, St. Louis, surrounded by brush, with an air of abandon in the streets, and a hospital that would disgrace even the name of "ruin." It went without saying that the colonial souls were in the same state of decay, in such a sad state that the Apostolic Prefect had left in despair. But Mother Javouhey and her sisters were not as easily discouraged.

The first contingent of six nuns set sail for Africa under the leadership of the youngest of the Javouhey sisters, Claudine, now known under her religious name of Mother Rosalie. Brother Pierre Javouhey also sailed at the same time, but his flesh was weak, and he soon gave up and returned to France. The nuns did not give up as easily. Administrative stupidity, dysentery, lack of money: none of these trifles could dislodge them from their chosen continent; particularly as they knew that Mother Javouhey was pulling strings in Paris to have a new Apostolic Prefect sent out, to say nothing of more medicines and other provisions.

The dear Mother was on her way to becoming a national character. The Duke Decazes lent his ear, and he was only one of several cabinet ministers. Cluny was overrun with applications for training for overseas service — so many that the Mother Superior could send reinforcements to Réunion and Senegal, as well as start new foundations in various parts of France, with enough left over to staff missions in Guadeloupe and Guiana. Whenever and wherever there was a roll call for the service of Christ, she was ready to answer, "Present."

All this was very fine, but it was still not her dream. She still dreamed of going in person to the Dark Continent to work. She carefully prepared for her departure so that the congregation would not suffer by her absence, and one fine morning she announced her plans to her sisters. Before they had time to object, she was aboard *La Panthère,* bound for St. Louis, in Senegal. The date was February 1,1822.

Her African period was for Mother Javouhey a time of happiness and fulfillment. Despite her countless difficulties, she had a feeling of really being where God wanted her to be. She also learned to know the natives. "I love the black peoples very much," she declared. "They are good, simple folk. Their only malice they get from us. It would not be difficult to convince them by example.

It was a shrewd judgment: Set the example. Make Christians of them. Henceforth this would be her goal, her only goal. And to attain it, she would love the blacks with a great love.

The steps this woman would have to take, the measures she would have to invent as prelude to her future achievements, are simply incredible. While the very great missionaries like St. Francis Xavier were pioneers and trailblazers, Mother Javouhey was also an architect and builder. She had a knack for overcoming obstacles. She knew how to give herself completely to a grand design.

"Let us be generous and open-hearted," she said. "Let there be no room for pettiness."

But unlike many idealists, she was far from impractical. Like the good Burgundian peasant that she was, she kept her feet on the ground. She bought no gold bricks.

Was the hospital run down? She had it renovated. Did the white colonials despise the blacks? Mother Javouhey decreed that in her presence and on her premises, all men were to be treated as equals, regardless of the color of their skin. Were colonial manners and morals deplorable? She would create her own colonies, agricultural colonies deep in the bush, where all farmers could live fraternally in decency and honesty, respecting Christian law and morality, sharing the products of the land they were cultivating. This woman of genius even evolved on her own an idea that St. Francis Xavier had conceived in

India but had never been able to bring to full fruition: the creation of a native clergy to spread the Gospel among men of their own race. To this end, she founded a seminary in France where young men of color could be sent and educated to become priests. Her fame spread throughout Africa. The English administrators of Sierra Leone invited her to carry on her work in that colony. She did so for two years.

But France was calling her. Her rapidly growing congregation was in need of her firm guidance. She had to agree to return home. When she sailed from St. Louis, more than a thousand blacks went to the port to see her off. It was a tumultuous crowd whose cheers were mingled with sobs. Some stooped to kiss her footprints. They all stood on the dock until the ship was out of sight, many of them weeping.

As long as she lived, the activity of Mother Javouhey was almost unimaginable. She was like a busy planter, sowing the good seed with full hands, right and left, day and night, without stopping: May the soil nurture it, and may the seed sprout! The Sisters of St. Joseph with their blue robes and their white plastrons were everywhere there was good to be done. They crossed the Atlantic to Guiana, to Martinique and Guadeloupe, and to the tiny isles of St. Pierre and Miquelon, off Newfoundland. They looked also to the East, where they landed at Pondichéry in French India in 1817. At home they were constantly busy, taking over the insane asylum at Rouen, founding establishments at Carcassonne, and nearby Chalabre and Limoux in the Aude; at Brest and Fontainebleau. And in the founder's home village of Chamblanc, which knew her as Nanette, two nuns carried on her very first work of teaching the catechism and also took care of her father, for Master Balthazar was now quite old and feeble.

The personal part played by Mother Javouhey in all this work was considerable. Always ready to take off for the four corners of the earth, this landlubber, born in the vineyards of Burgundy, seemed never happy except at sea. And her happiness aboard ship was not physical, for she was always seasick. But, as she once said between two spells of mortal torment, "I am no more afraid of the sea and its sickness than I am of the land."

"My most seasoned sailor," Admiral Tréhouart called her one stormy day at sea aboard his ship, as she was making her rounds. Martinique, Guadeloupe, St. Pierre and Miquelon, the Indies, Madagascar, Oceania, or the islands of the Indian Ocean, Nossi-Bé and Mayotte in the Comoro Archipelago — the planet must have seemed very small for this indefatigable woman who ran up a log of nearly thirty-five thousand miles by sea, forty thousand by land.

Perhaps the most impressive of her long list of successes was her work on the Mana River in French Guiana. The Mana flows into the Atlantic a little to the south of the Maroni, the principal river of this little-known but ill-famed country. There is nothing very pleasant about Guiana. Its year-round humid, tropical heat is unhealthful; its pouring rains measure 120 inches in six months; the high grass of its savannahs swarms with snakes and vicious insects. Rubber and rosewood, manioc and bananas are its principal resources, apart from the gold, which dubious adventurers come to seek in the sand of its rivers. The picture would not seem propitious to the work of a congregation of nuns.

Mother Javouhey, however, seemed to thrive on obstacles. The country was difficult? Fine. There would be that much more work to be done. She was not likely to be received with open arms by the mixture of Europeans, Negroes, and Indians who lived in Guiana without faith or law? Still better, since the Christ had said that the lost sheep deserved the greatest care. So when the government asked her to establish a foundation in Guiana, the courageous woman accepted without question.

She immediately drew up a report in which she outlined a project similar to the one she had organized in Senegal, but with some improvements. She would found a model colony of farmers and artisans brought from France. They would live in a fraternal community with orphans, carefully chosen and raised, who would be the future settlers destined to renew the population of the country. Those willing to join her in the great adventure would sign on for three years, during which time they would be fed, housed, clothed, and given medical care by the enterprise. In addition, each would receive a cash allotment of three hundred gold francs a year (equal to about two hundred thousand francs of mid-twentieth century French currency). The resourceful woman foresaw every contingency and organized accordingly.

On June 26, 1828, the *Bretonne* and the *Ménagère* sailed from the port of Brest with an expedition of more than one hundred persons under the personal command of Mother

Javouhey. The party included nine nuns, twenty-seven lay sisters, thirty-nine colonists (with five wives and eleven children), and twelve workers. They were to take over land along the banks of the Mana that had been abandoned after two previous attempts at colonization.

Nothing, or almost nothing, remained of the previous projects, both government-sponsored. The last fifteen of the settlers had "gone native," and the jungle had reclaimed the land they had tried to cultivate. All that was left were the fifteen abandoned houses, which were rapidly disintegrated in the damp rot of the tropics. Here was Mother Javouhey's starting point.

A year after the expedition had landed, the surrounding land had been cleared again and planted with bananas and manioc. Livestock grazed in fenced-in pastures. A new port had sprung up, with docks and a shipyard that was handling a surprising amount of commerce. A church, which was extravagantly called "the cathedral," rose above the houses of the colonists.

The whole community and its nuns lived a happy, well-disciplined life that amazed visitors. Everyone went to Mass on Sundays; there was community prayer in the evening. There was no need of gendarmes or policemen. Officials from St.-Laurent du Maroni, the capital of French Guiana and the seat of the notorious penal colony, did not believe their eyes or ears. This crew of workers, which now included Indians, blacks, and white men whom it would not be prudent to ask for identity papers, obeyed the Mother Superior like well-behaved children.

This utopian situation did not last very long, however. The French revolution of 1830, which re-established the monarchy and put Louis Philippe on the throne, had disastrous consequences for Mana. The new government took little interest in the colonial experiment, and the community spirit flagged. Some of the original settlers left the colony to try their hand on their own.

Mother Javouhey concentrated her efforts on the orphans as her hope for the future. When slavery was abolished throughout the French Empire in 1831, she agreed to make Mana into a kind of school-haven where ex-slaves could be educated and reoriented for five or six years. At Mana, they could serve what amounted to an apprenticeship for liberty before going out on their own as free men. As usual, Mother Javouhey was thinking in terms of a grand design. She would bring women from Africa, so that the freed slaves could start families. She would create new all-black villages with one man or woman as administrator and protector of each. It was a grandiose plan, but it had the backing of an influential figure in the government: the poet Lamartine, at the time a cabinet minister.

The blacks did indeed begin arriving at Mana. New villages did arise, governed by the Christian way of life as before. And the liturgical ceremonies brought together with the same enthusiasm white colonials, black ex-slaves, and the self-effacing nuns. When the people asked Mother Jahouvey what she had done to achieve a thousand times more success than all the administrators of Guiana with their gendarmes and their prisons, she replied with her best smile, "I just acted like a mother among her children."

∞

Thus was this woman of God a worthy rival of the greatest of missionaries. Anyone watching her at work would find it hard to decide which of her many qualities was the most admirable: her audacity, her spirit of resolve, or her virile qualities of organization and command. When she returned to France, recalled by the prodigious growth of her institute, and her need to see firsthand all the new foundations being sought in the four corners of the earth, she was a celebrity. The newspapers praised her. People pointed her out in the street: a robust nun in blue with pink cheeks and eyes that laughed in the shadow of her headdress. Passersby greeted her. King Louis Philippe, after carefully studying her accomplishments, said of her, "Mother Javouhey? She's a great man."

During the darkest days of 1848, when violence again broke out in the streets of Paris, the disorders provided new measures of her popularity. At the first news of the riots, she hurried to the scene, ready to help where she could, to calm troubled spirits and care for the wounded. She found the streets of the capital obstructed by barricades on which armed men stood ready to open fire. Tranquilly she went from barricade to barricade, her coif floating in the wind and the big cross of the Mother Superior knocking against her white plastron. The insurgent workers recognized her. They had heard about Mana and her inexhaustible works of charity. They greeted her by name: "It's Mother Javouhey!" They cheered her as she appeared, joked with her as she left. "It's General Javouhey! Pass, General!"

And Mother Javouhey passed, smiling at the same barricades where Monsignor Denis Affre, the Archbishop of Paris, was to fall mortally wounded while on a mission of peace on June 24.

The people in her beloved Mana did not forget her while she was so far away. Her invisible presence seemed to keep order in the little colony. When the Republic of 1848 decreed that Mana should be a free borough with administrative equality with all French Communes, the ex-slaves rebelled. They wanted their nuns to continue the administration of Mana. It was Mother Isabelle, the founder's representative, who restored order. And when they were told to elect a deputy to Parliament, Mana voted unanimously for Mother Javouhey. When it was explained to the electorate that under the Republic women were not eligible to hold office, spokesmen for Mana then declared that they would not vote at all.

It must not be thought that such an enterprise was accomplished without trouble. All great works carry within themselves the seeds of misunderstanding, distrust, and jealousy. Mother Javouhey, who had never had any illusions about men, learned the truth the hard way. How many times did she butt her head against official stupidity, red tape, and the ill will of those whose private sordid interests she might cross!

But the most serious of her ordeals came from the Church herself, the Church she served so splendidly, the Church that, on October 15, 1850, was to raise her to the altar. One of the contemporary representatives of the Church was to prove himself as unjust and as misunderstanding as man can be. He was the Bishop of Autun, a Msgr. d'Héricourt, an ex-army officer who was well along in years when he took the vows, and who spoke from his episcopal throne with the authoritarian voice of a cavalry captain. On the pretext that Cluny, mother convent of the Sisters of St. Joseph, was within his diocese, he claimed control of the congregation.

Mother Javouhey was too much aware of the worldwide problems and her own involvement in them to accept without blinking the interference of a provincial prelate from his backwater bishopric in the Morvan. A terrific dispute ensued. In high dudgeon against what he called a "mutineer," the Bishop of Autun went so far as to persuade the Apostolic Prefect of Guiana to deny Mother Javouhey the holy sacraments! It is not difficult to imagine what a shock this extreme measure was to a saintly soul who lived only for God; and with what anguish she watched her girls, her sister nuns, approach the Communion table from which she was excluded! In this moment of deep affliction, the woman of action also showed herself to be a true mystic, a soul aglow with light.

"I have only Thee, Lord," she prayed. "Which is why I throw myself into Thy arms, begging Thee not to abandon Thy child."

So she emerged from the ordeal greater than before. Not a word of anger escaped her lips against the bishop who had misjudged her. "We must pray for him as for a benefactor," she told her sisters, "for he has given us the opportunity to suffer."

When Msgr. d'Héricourt died in 1851, he and Mother Javouhey were more or less reconciled, although he was distrustful of her until the end. On learning of his death, she said gently, with perhaps just a hint of Burgundian roguishness,

"The good Monsignor has preceded me. This is as it should be. All honor to whom honor is due." And she added that she would pray daily for his soul.

Mother Javouhey was herself failing in health. She was too ill to go to Rome later that year to receive the solemn approval of the Pope for her institute. She grew weaker day by day. On July 15, she died, characteristically as she had lived: simply and decisively, abruptly, without long-drawn-out agony.

She left behind her some nine hundred nuns scattered throughout the world. As I write this, they number more than 3,500, divided among 269 branches, all faithful heirs of her to whom the black race is deeply indebted for a lifelong fight for racial equality, and to whom Christian history owes one of its most living pages: Mother Javouhey, that "great man."

Hermit of the Sahara

Late in the morning of March 6, 1897, a stranger knocked at the door of the convent of the Clarist Sisters in Nazareth and asked to be hired as a gardener. The nun in attendance was startled. The man's long hooded blouse of blue and white stripes, his faded cotton trousers, clumsily wrapped turban, and dusty, down-at-the-heel sandals gave him the appearance of a beggar rather than a gardener. But he spoke impeccable French, and there was a serene dignity about the scrawny, dark little man with the bright, deep-set eyes that was impressive.

"The Franciscan Fathers at Jaffa told me your community was looking for a gardener, Sister, so I came," he said. Then he added, "Today is St. Colette's Day, isn't it?"

The good sister smiled. Anyone so well spoken and who knew of St. Colette, the great reformer of the Clarist Sisters, must be a man of God.

The strange visitor seemed to be even more a man of God when, having asked permission to enter the chapel, he remained in silent, motionless adoration before the crucifix for more than three hours. He did not even notice the good sister who came from time to time to look at him with admiration mixed with uneasy amazement. At last the nun went to report to the Mother Superior.

"I know." Mother St. Michel smiled gently. "Don't disturb him. When he has finished his orisons, take him to the lodge at the end of the garden, and see that he is comfortably settled."

But there were more surprises in store for the little nun. She could not get the new gardener settled in the neat little lodge provided for him, because he refused to stay there. He wanted nothing better than a lonely close at the edge of town. He would take no bed, no mattress, and no bedding — and the spring nights are cool in Galilee. When she spoke of his meals, and how they would be served, he merely shook his head and smiled. A handful of cracked grain and water would be ample, he declared.

Soon everyone in the community and in the little town of Nazareth was talking about the "mysterious gardener," who lived as austerely as the earliest hermits. At whatever hour of the night he awoke, he began his prayers. When the *Angelus*[21] rang from the many churches that dotted both slopes of the little valley, he could be seen making his way through the half-light of dawn to the Convent of St. Francis, where he told his Rosary until six o'clock. Then he went on to the Clarist

---

[21] At six o'clock a.m., noon, and six o'clock p.m., some churches ring a bell to call the faithful to pray the *Angelus*, a prayer that recalls the Incarnation.

Sisters, swept out the chapel, and made everything ready for Mass. All day long, he busied himself with his chores, repairing a wall, spading up the kitchen garden, or going to the post with the letters. What a marvelous servitor the Clarists had found!

When he had a moment of rest, he hurried to the chapel to pray, worship, and meditate. And if he was far from town when he paused to rest, his lips would be seen to move as he contemplated the rustic scene: the dark spires of cyprus rising above the gray-green of the olive trees, the brilliant purple of the bougainvillea covering the walls. "We have a saint in our house," the nuns said to one another. The Mother Superior, who had been briefed by the Franciscans of Jaffa, smiled without comment.

Asking the gardener himself who he was would have been a waste of time. Strange and contradictory rumors circulated around the man, but nobody dreamed of questioning him. Some said he was a former Trappist father who had come to Nazareth to find even more complete solitude; others that he was a French army officer. The gardener spoke to no one except in the line of duty. One day at the post office, a gossipy businessman asked indiscreetly whether it was true that in France he had "held the position of count." The gardener's warm smile reappeared on his thin, bearded face as he replied, "I am an old soldier."

Seemingly he had no other aim in life than to put into practice the famous words from Thomas à Kempis's *Imitation of Christ*: "Aspire to be unknown and held as nothing." If the people of Nazareth had been able to peep into the notebooks where he inscribed his daily observations, they might have read such thoughts as "It was in the hour of greatest annihilation that Jesus saved the world" and "Jesus had so firmly seized the highest seat that no one has been able to snatch it from Him."

Who could have guessed that the brown tunic and apron of the gardener of the Clarist Sisters was hiding, known to God alone, a former lieutenant of the Fourth Regiment, Chasseurs d'Afrique, Viscount Charles de Foucauld.

∞

If ever a man was recaptured by the Lord by main force — as St. Paul and Ramon Lull had been — it was the big, lazy, boastful, and dissipated second lieutenant of Hussars at Pont-à-Mousson, who, at the age of twenty-three, thought life consisted of astonishing the little Lorraine town by his wild spending and extravagant behavior. Orphaned at eight, badly brought up by an indulgent grandfather, he was a miserable student and was admitted to the St. Cyr military academy by the skin of his teeth. He had early lost all faith and piety and most of his moral sense. Throwing his money away right and left, dressing with ridiculous affectation, always running off to Paris in quest of sorry pleasures, he seemed dedicated to the idea of presenting himself in the worst light possible.

In 1880, however, a fortuitous circumstance brought him to his senses and convinced him that he was made of better stuff than he was displaying. His regiment, now become the Fourth African Chasseurs, had been thrown into combat against an Algerian chieftain who had declared holy war against the French in the country south of Oran. Foucauld, who was twenty-three at the time, was on leave and having a high time at the Lake Geneva resort of Evian. Descended from a soldier of St. Louis, the young lieutenant felt his warrior's blood stir in him at the news that his regiment was in action. Leaving behind him the casino, the beach, and the gaming table, he rushed off to Africa, got back into uniform, and rejoined his troop.

The campaign, which was hard-fought on difficult terrain, revealed the lad as an energetic and courageous leader, capable of enduring great fatigue cheerfully, and taking care of his men with skill and consideration. The soldier had displaced the playboy in him, and Africa — austere, uncompromising Africa — had begun to work its imperious fascination on him.

And it was to be a lifelong relationship. For those who know her, the Dark Continent has a charm all her own. Her wide horizons, the stark nakedness of her desert landscapes, the flashing splendor of her blue, palm-clustered oases, and, stretched above her cruel vastness, her great canopy of hard blue sky and her star-powdered nights: all this is the stuff of dreams and grips the soul with irresistible power. All those who had been exposed to the charms of Africa have fallen in love with her.

Charles de Foucauld was one of them. When the rebellion had been put down, he resolved to devote himself to knowing Africa and to making Africa known. At this time, one of the least-explored parts was Morocco, a country where Europeans were so unfavorably received that to deviate from the official itinerary known as "Ambassadors' Road," by which accredited envoys traveled to reach the Sultan's capitals, was to risk death. Charles de Foucauld decided to explore this mysterious land. To this end he learned Arabic and disguised himself as a Jewish merchant. He was accompanied by a real Jew togged out in a garnet-red caftan as long as a cassock and wearing a red fez surrounded by a turban. The Jew's name was Mardo-chée, and it developed that he was not quite trustworthy. Foucauld himself was so well disguised in a Syrian tunic, Turk-ish vest, linen breeches, and turban that some old comrades he ran into in Sétif, as he was preparing to leave Algeria, did not recognize him.

He entered Morocco through Tetuán in June 1883, and was to remain until May 1884. With the boldness of youth — he was then twenty-six — he penetrated into parts of the country never before seen by a European. Sometimes accepted at face value, sometimes suspected and barely escaping with his life, often aided by local chiefs, he traveled two thousand miles, crossing the country in all directions, making notes and sketches, studying Moroccan geography, customs, and arts, constantly bedazzled by the beauty and richness of the still unknown country. In many places, he found pro-French senti-ment. He heard such things as "When are the French com-ing?" and "Why don't the French come in and establish order, stop banditry, and end the intertribal wars?"

His zigzag course took him through Taza, Fez, Sefrou, Bou-el-Djad, the Tadla, then Tikrit and Tisint, bringing him at last to Mogador, dirty, wan, exhausted, and with an empty purse. The doorman at the French consulate would not believe him when he said he was a French cavalry officer. The medal bestowed upon him by the Geographical Society for his two books describing his exploration was well earned.

Certainly a life of action and adventure was infinitely better than his early years of indolence and dissipation. Africa had restored to Charles de Foucauld his dignity as a man, and had taught him the discipline of effort, which he had not known in his youth. But it did even more. One thing the traveler had discovered in Morocco was religious faith. If there is one specimen of humanity that the Moslem despises and rejects, it is the man who believes in nothing. A man without religion, to the Moslem, is lower than a dog.

Islam may be a doctrine tainted with error, much inferior to the Christian revelation, but the great merit of those who are faithful to it is that they put its principles scrupulously into practice. They take their religion seriously. After watching the devout Moslems ritually saying their prayers thrice daily, after talking with Marabouts and with learned and respected doctors of Koranic law, Charles de Foucauld began to wonder whether he, a son of Christians — he was the descendant of a Crusader, of soldiers of Joan of Arc,[22] of a family that counted a priest martyred during the Revolution — was not betraying a great ideal in living a life of disbelief and in denying God. Under his differing identities — the sorry externals of a dissipated army officer, the more respectable personality of a brave explorer — he still possessed a generous soul that had

---

[22] St. Joan of Arc (1412-1431), French heroine who led the French army against English invaders and was burned to death for alleged heresy, but later declared innocent.

remained intact, thirsty for nobility. God had already won the first skirmish.

Back in France, Foucauld was completely bewildered. He no longer felt at home. So he returned to Africa, this time headed for the Sahara by way of Laghouat, an oasis in southern Algeria, the mysterious settlements grouped around the oasis of Mzab — Ghardaïa and El Goléa — returning by way of Gabès and the salt lagoons of Tunisia. For the first time, he discovered the loneliness of the great desert, the slow advances on the trails, the silence broken only by the monotonous sighing of the wind. Meditating to the rhythmic tread of a camel, he thought of Him who had ordered the universe, who had set the stars in their courses, and who was more immutable than the immutable spaces of the desert and the desert skies. He thought of the Eternal. Inner voices spoke to him in a language he was not sure he could understand.

Once more in Paris, a chance — which we may well believe was a medium of Providence — brought him face-to-face with an extraordinary priest, regarded by many of his faithful as a saint. Abbé Huvelin, curate of the Church of St. Augustine, was still a young man, but he was frail and sickly in appearance, with wrinkled skin and limbs twisted by rheumatism. His wasted face, however, glowed with the Light. A graduate of the Higher Normal School, he not only was a saintly soul, but he had a keen mind and a well-trained intellect. A relative spoke to Foucauld of this priest, and the inner voice immediately advised the soldier-explorer, "Go! He is expecting you."

Docilely he obeyed.

"Monsieur l'Abbé," he said to the curate, "I am without faith, but I would like instruction in the Catholic religion."

"Kneel," said the priest, "and confess your sins."

"I . . . I am without faith," Foucauld repeated, stammering. The brawling braggart of an ex-cavalry officer was overawed by the commanding presence of the priest.

"Confess," ordered the priest.

And Charles de Foucauld confessed. It was a morning shortly before Easter of 1888.

"Have you had breakfast?" the priest then asked. On receiving a negative reply, he said, "Then go into the church at once. Mass is about to begin. You will approach the Communion table."

Thus it happened that, at the age of thirty, Charles de Foucauld received what he himself called his "second first Communion."

Fifteen months later, in a wild corner of the Ardèche Plateau, swept by the Mistral and spattered with snow, a man made his way to the Abbey of Notre-Dame des Neiges, a man whose life had at last found its direction. Viscount Charles de Foucauld, wearing the white cowl of the Sons of St. Bernard,[23] would henceforth and forever renounce the world and his mad youth, and would expiate his sins.

But could Trappist discipline make him forget Africa and the men he had known there — honest, decent men but living in ignorance of Christian truth? Was not another destiny awaiting him?

---

[23] St. Bernard (1090-1153), abbot of Clairvaux.

Heroes of God

∞

The life of the Trappist is neither pleasant nor comfortable: arising in the dark of night, long Divine Offices, hard manual labor, severe fasting. Many great souls deem its renunciations sufficient to lead to God. Saints, however, have their own exacting needs, and what may suit an ordinary Christian would strike them as too little.

Leaving the Trappists and burying himself in the total destitution and complete solitude we saw at Nazareth, Charles de Foucauld had taken the road that God Himself had indicated, and which he would follow to the end, to martyrdom.

However, his desire "to be unknown and held as nothing" was to be put to the test. The Mother Superior of the Clarist Sisters of Jerusalem, to whom the Nazareth community was responsible, was a remarkable woman of uncommon energy and intelligence. She came to see the hermit gardener of whom she had heard so much and, soon after meeting him, recognized in him a creature with a mission from God. Here was a man, she thought, who should become a priest, to do more good to more souls, to be truly a conqueror for the Holy Spirit. But to the friendly suggestion of Mother Elisabeth, Br. Charles replied, "To be a priest I would have to show myself. I am made for a hidden life."

It took many exhortations and remonstrances to overcome the stubbornness of this disciple of humility. Luckily, his dear friend and guide, Abbé Huvelin, shared Mother Elisabeth's opinion, and Foucauld gave in. He went back to France and re-entered the Trappist abbey, to recall his first steps in the tracks of the Christ. He prepared himself for the priesthood with fervor and austerity that won the admiration of all the monks. In June 1901, he was ordained by Monsignor the Bishop of Viviers in the Ardèche.

What was to be his next step? He would not remain with the Trappists; they represented for him just one stage. Nor could he return to Nazareth, for the good Clarist Sisters could scarcely employ a priest as a servant. But during the retreats while he was preparing for his ordination, he had felt a strong force that seemed to emanate from God pushing him toward a new destiny, toward the selfsame sick, the lost sheep for whom the Lord reserved His tenderest care. Charles de Foucauld knew thousands of souls abandoned far from the truth, yet who deserved to receive it. He would go to the thousands of Moslems in Morocco, to the seven or eight million in the Sahara, his arms outstretched, offering them the Christ. And he would choose the Sahara, rather than Morocco, because his task there would be more difficult.

His mind was made up. He would find some military outpost in the desert without a chaplain. There he would be the witness, the spokesman for the Christ, in the midst of natives who had never heard the Good Tidings.

"That land and those souls have been awaiting the Gospel for nineteen hundred years," he told himself as he studied the vast open spaces on the map, dotted here and there by a few oases. He would bring it to them.

The method that he had conceived and would put into operation was different from that used by the admirable White Fathers founded by Cardinal Lavigerie. Foucauld took his inspiration from the hermits of the fifth and sixth centuries of our era who, like the celebrated St. Anthony,[24] were living examples of Christian saintliness in the deserts of Egypt and Syria, and to whom, little by little, the people flocked. He, too, would lead the silent life of a monk in a sort of hermitage, demonstrating to the Moslems what a true Christian was like, loving them and serving them in humility and the gentleness of poverty. Even the worst of them, the most brutal, would have the right to his pity, for no one is excluded from the mercy of Christ. His house would be open to all, to anyone who would hear him speak of Heaven and the kingdom of God.

He put his plan into operation immediately. As soon as he had secured the necessary authorizations from his superiors and from the military authorities, he sailed for Algeria. From Oran, he pushed southward, carrying with him only a few crates containing the necessary materials for erecting an oratory. As he passed through the military posts of the south, many of the officers were startled to see their former comrade in arms, the natty Lieutenant Charles de Foucauld, dressed as a poor Bedouin and living off an occasional handful of dates and a cup of water.

He settled at Beni-Abbès, far beyond Figig and Colomb-Béchar, on the edge of the great Erg, that desolate sea of sand. Four companies were garrisoned there in a small fort perched on a cliff overlooking the oasis. Fr. de Foucauld refused to live

---

[24] St. Anthony (251-356), desert monk and father of Western monasticism.

under the shelter of their guns. Neither would he be domiciled in the palm groves of the oasis, among the lovely cool gardens, the peach and fig orchards. All he needed was a patch of sand among the pink dunes. He would dig his own well there to get water. With a few beams, a few stones he had gathered, and a little mud mixed with straw, he soon raised the walls of his chapel. And Fr. de Foucauld was in business.

The natives — half blacks, half Arabs — were greatly intrigued by the newcomer. They heard him singing at night, a little off-key but with great fervor, projecting the verses of the Psalms into the desert silence. Like the old Trappist that he was, Fr. de Foucauld arose at midnight, rang his little bell, and set about chanting the Divine Office. His austere way of life excited great admiration. The natives noted that he ate almost nothing, prayed constantly, and slept little. One day, a sharpshooter who was visiting him remarked that his cell was too small for him to stretch out comfortably to sleep. He replied simply, "Did Jesus stretch out comfortably on the Cross?" The Moslems admitted to each other that in all Islam they had never seen a Marabout more saintly than this *Roumi*.

His charity knew no limits. Everything he owned was at the disposition of others. His white cowl, a souvenir of Trappist days, was in rags. Somebody, he never knew who, sent him a bolt of fine white wool. Instead of making a new robe for himself, he dressed several black children. Money that his family sent him he used to buy freedom for slaves. Very likely he hoped that his protégés would accept Christianity, but he was often disappointed. Frequently the slaves he had freed, instead of trying to follow his example, became poor idlers

Heroes of God

without great hope. But Fr. de Foucauld was not easily discouraged. He would do his own job and let God take care of the rest. A few baptisms, chiefly children, almost no adults: a poor harvest, at least on the surface, for such a great effort.

His real reward was the affection and respect he had won from the natives, both nomads and villagers, for hundreds of miles around. From camp to camp, and from oasis to oasis, the French Marabout of Beni-Abbès was a subject of conversation. His thin figure, almost lost in his white gandurah, circled at the waist by a leather belt on which he had sewed a red cloth heart surmounted by a cross, was a familiar sight. Once a *rezzou* of Moroccans from the Tafilelt crossed the border to attack Taghit. The French moved in to repulse the raid, and Fr. de Foucauld rode out after them alone in hostile territory seething with unrest, simply to care for the wounded. The radiance of the man was so great that the most violent Bedouin did not dare attack him.

∞

And yet the hermit of Beni-Abbès was not satisfied. Life a few hundred yards from a French outpost seemed too protected, too comfortable. He was in the desert, true, but he was not in the heart of the desert, not in the most forsaken, the wildest part. He must go further. "When I dream, the horizons of the desert beckon to me."

So new plans took shape, plans to penetrate deeper into old Africa, where he could create a new community, a brotherhood, an order, "The Little Brothers of the Sacred Heart." He and his brothers would be God's vanguard. "The more numerous and the more fervent this silent vanguard, the sooner the hour of overt preaching will strike."

Providence was still watching. Providence again made the decision. One day Charles de Foucauld was visited in his hermitage by the commander-in-chief of all French oasis outposts, Major Laperrine. No one knew the desert better or loved it more than the major, who had crossed it in all directions and who was fated to die there of thirst, after an airplane crash years later. The hermit and the military man were old comrades in arms, and they talked at length of the vastness of Africa: of the oases of Gouara, of Touat, and Tidikelt, and of the mountains of Hoggar farther on, where the Tuaregs lived, and where the White Fathers had not yet been able to send missionaries. Why didn't Fr. de Foucauld go himself?

The decision was almost immediate, although it was not an easy one to make. Fr. de Foucauld would leave many friends and protégés behind in Beni-Abbès if he set forth on another adventure. But a voice deep within him told him that down there, in the far-off solitude, God was calling him.

He left Beni-Abbès in January 1904. When his superior, the Vicar Apostolic of the Sahara, asked him if he was really prepared to go to work among the Tuaregs, he replied that he was "ready to leave for the end of the world and live there until the Last Judgment," wherever there was a need to preach the Gospel. The Hoggar, where he was going, might just as well have been at the end of the earth — a mountainous plateau crossed by steep ranges and wild valleys, most of which had never been explored by Europeans. The Tuaregs who lived there were white Berbers, big, handsome men with pale eyes.

Heroes of God

They were fierce warriors, who often came out of their mountains armed with lances, sabers, and shields, riding their mehari
racing camels to attack and rob some distant caravan. The
veils they wore across the lower half of the face as protection
against wind-blown sand made their sullen features seem even
more mysterious. On several occasions, they had attacked and
decimated columns of French troops. At this very moment in
1904, they were seeking an accord with the French, and one of
their principal chiefs had gone to In Salah, the capital of the
region, to make contact with French officials. It was an oppor-
tune moment, and Fr. de Foucauld seized it.

By long, difficult stages, Fr. de Foucauld moved toward the
new country he was to win for God: Adrar, Akabli, In Salah.
He was in a state of constant excitement, and his ever-alert
curiosity was at work noting down features of geography, customs, and agriculture. His heart exulted at the thought of the
tasks ahead. A single shadow darkened his spirits: he had not
succeeded in founding the fraternity he had been dreaming of.
He would never succeed. (Two candidates who were to show
interest would withdraw when they learned how strict the regulations were and how hard the life in prospect.) What differ-
ence? Here again, he would put his trust in God.

For weeks on end, accompanied by a lieutenant and a few
men, the father traveled through the unknown country without incident. The Tuaregs showed no suspicion of this humble
visitor dressed as a poor Bedouin. He began to know the people, to pick up their language, and to distinguish between their
three classes: the Haratins, freed ex-slaves who cultivated the
fields in the valleys; the middle classes, who managed the

Hermit of the Sahara

trade and commerce; and the nobles, shepherds, and warriors. The *Aménokal,* the supreme chief of all the Tuareg tribes, received the missionary cordially.

Of the twenty places he was considering as a spot to settle, he finally chose a village at the south of the massif, a cluster of huts a mile above sea level, far from the main roads, where, as he himself wrote, "there would never be a garrison, a telegraph office, a European, or, for a long time, a mission." He could not suspect that his presence there would make this forsaken corner of Africa a name known to the Christians of all the world: Tamanrasset.

His total isolation here was awesome. The squad that had accompanied him had gone back. He was a thousand miles from Beni-Abbès, more than four hundred miles from In Salah. The hermit was completely alone with the natives, without contact with France, save for a chance caravan, without possibility of outside help, material or spiritual. "To do my utmost for salvation of the infidel peoples of these lands, in total oblivion of myself," he wrote in his notes the day of his arrival. Total oblivion of self! What could be more necessary to one seeking to testify for Christ among men of violence and cruelty, among men driven by covetousness of all kinds, among barbarians? And what weapons are at the disposition of the saint? He lists them himself: uniquely, prayer and penitence. It is by example that he would win their hearts.

And the miracle came to pass. As at Beni-Abbès, he built his hermitage, a group of miserable huts, with the materials of the country. As in Beni-Abbès, he slept on a wattle of reeds, and he ate a nauseating porridge of barley meal and crushed dates. His routine? Up at midnight, long services, prayers, and charity calls. He spoke to farmers. He cared for the sick. He taught the women to sew with steel needles. Little by little, people started coming to see him — to ask his advice, to have him arbitrate a quarrel or prescribe a remedy. To all of them he spoke of God in simple words, and they listened. The role he played at Beni-Abbès he repeated again in the heart of the Hoggar massif and with the same happy success.

Nine years were to pass in this manner — nine years of silence and obscure work. There were few outstanding incidents in so many days of saintly patience. The departure of an early convert, Paul, whose health was failing almost prevented him from saying Mass; fortunately, authorization to celebrate the Sacrifice without a lay assistant arrived in time, so the solitary hermit could continue his great consolation. Once he nearly died from the sting of a horned viper (there were so many in the neighborhood that he had to build a thirty-inch doorsill to keep them out of the hermitage) and underwent the terrible Tuareg remedy of having the wound cauterized with a red-hot iron. Another time when death threatened — he was so exhausted by fasting and overwork that he was having frequent fainting spells — he was saved by his old friend Major Laperrine, who sent him provisions and ordered him to eat.

He made three very brief visits to France. On the last trip, he was accompanied by a young tribal chief who on his return would report to his people on what he had seen in Europe. But the hermit was never happy in his own country. He had scarcely landed before he began thinking of going back.

Africa, fascinating Africa, was his horizon now. His true destiny was with those he had come to love as his own.

In 1913, France moved into the Hoggar for good. Forts were built, military garrisons established. All commanding officers had orders to consult the Hermit of Tamanrasset, the man who knew more about the wild massif than anyone in the world. Wasn't this unarmed hermit the veritable spiritual head of the country? The natives themselves came from miles around to ask his advice. His name was on every tongue, from tent to tent, from tribe to tribe. He had not made many conversions to Christ, true. But had he not himself declared that he was only the vanguard of the Lord? He had given his testimony. He had taught these men who knew nothing of Christ the meaning of a servant of His Word. That was sufficient. The first furrow had been plowed. The field would be next.

∞

On September 7, 1914, Fr. de Foucauld was to have celebrated the ninth anniversary of his first Mass in Tamanrasset. The officers and men garrisoned at nearby Fort Motylinski would be there. They loved him and admired him. The military courier who made the round trip to In Salah twice a month always stopped at his Hermitage de la Fraternité on the way. The Tuaregs, too, would celebrate the anniversary, for their own *Aménokal* rarely made a decision without consulting the French priest.

Tamanrasset, perhaps because of Fr. de Foucauld's presence there, had developed phenomenally. The village had been rebuilt, brick houses had sprung up, and a road had been begun.

Heroes of God

An experimental radio transmitter had been erected and communication established with the Eiffel Tower station in Paris. The hermit, however, had not changed. He still wore his white robe with the cross superimposed on a red heart, still the same old sandals, and a kepi without a visor, or a badly knotted headcloth.

Suddenly, on September 3 came the terrible news: War! Europe was aflame. France was invaded. Charles de Foucauld, the ex-cavalry officer, volunteered to return to the service, even though he was now fifty-six years old. He was ordered to stay put — where his presence alone was enough to ensure the tranquillity of a restless people. He himself realized that he was of greater use to his country in Africa than in France. The tribes of the Sahara had submitted to France because France was strong. Would they continue loyal if France were defeated, even momentarily, and French troops had to be withdrawn from Africa?

The Germans, too, realized the vulnerability of France in Africa and acted accordingly. German agents and German arms found their way to the tribes of most violent temperament and dubious loyalties. From the Fezzan in southern Libya, bands of *fellagahs* armed with German rifles attacked southern Tunisia in the winter of 1914-15 and were repulsed. France, however, took precautions in the Hoggar. Early in 1916, a small fort was erected at Tamanrasset, large enough to contain the civil population within its crenelated bastions in case of attack. Danger threatened. *Fellagahs* were reported on the move in the region. Fr. de Foucauld agreed to come and live inside the fort after sending to the mountains all the women, children, and old men of the village. The old soldier himself could withstand a siege, in case of attack, since such was his duty. His duty! Deep in his heart he had but one desire: to spill his blood on this patch of African soil, to offer himself in holocaust so that God should save the souls of his people.

God's response came on December 1. Night was closing in. Fr. de Foucauld was alone in the little fort. His lay brother was on an errand in the village, a few hundred yards away. There came a knock at the door. The hermit followed the long narrow corridor, built so that it could be blocked by one man. He challenged: "Who's there?"

"Courier from Fort Motylinski," came the reply.

The priest recognized the voice: a Haratin of the village. He opened the gate. Someone seized his arm and dragged him outside. He was surrounded by a mob of maniacs, howling at the smell of victory. The traitor had done his work well.

The mob swarmed into the fort, sacking and pillaging. Bound hand and foot, Fr. de Foucauld lay in a corner of his tiny chapel, watching the vandals destroy the liturgical books and the sacred vessels as he waited for death. The *fellagahs* questioned him — in vain. "When is the convoy due? Are there soldiers in the village?"

Fr. de Foucauld remained silent, praying. His eyes were already looking beyond his approaching suffering to the hope of happiness that already glowed in his heart.

Suddenly two camel drivers entered the fort, the real couriers from Fort Motylinski. They fell under a hail of bullets. This was too much for Fr. de Foucauld. He made an effort to rise and bring succor to the two dying men. One of the three men guarding him pointed his gun at him and pulled the trigger. The bullet entered his head behind the right ear and came out the left. The man of God collapsed without uttering a sound.

It was the first Friday in December, a day dedicated to the Sacred Heart.

Bl. Damien

∞

Missionary to Lepers

In the heart of the Pacific, thousands of miles from land, the Hawaiian Archipelago drops its chaplet of islands like flowers plucked from a garland and left to float upon the waves. The warm, humid air, saturated with rain, encourages a lush vegetation there; coconuts, sugar cane, pineapples, and other tropical fruits grow in profusion. The flowers are more dazzling than anywhere else in the world. Handsome dark-skinned men and women live in what is almost a perpetual vacation, singing, dancing, playing the guitar, adorning themselves with chains of jasmine blossoms. Even the waves seem to dance gaily as they break on the white coral beaches, lightly speeding along the frail outrigger canoes. Hawaii, Pearl of the Pacific, where the names of islands and cities tinkle like strings of seashells: Maui, Oahu, Lanai, Niihau, Honolulu.

A paradise — a paradise on earth it would be, were it not for the volcanoes scattered through the archipelago, volcanoes whose gaping maws are ever ready to spew forth lava, whose terrible awakening splits the earth and crushes houses while man and nature howl together in panic. A paradise, yes, but continually menaced by hell.

On May 4, 1873, on the island of Maui, near the center of the archipelago, six priests met with the Vicar Apostolic of Hawaii, Monsignor Maigret, pioneer of the evangelical task, who thirty years earlier had come halfway around the world to bring the islanders the Word of God. The six younger men were all missionaries under his authority, all belonging to the Congregation of the Sacred Hearts of Jesus and Mary. The congregation was founded during the reign of revolutionary terror eighty years earlier by Fr. Coudrin in the rue de Picpus in Paris; the street gave its name to the members who are commonly called "Picpuciens."

The meeting in Maui was for a ceremonial, the consecration of a new church. So the missionaries wore, instead of the shabby cassocks of their daily work, white robes ornamented with two embroidered hearts and the mantle similar to that of the Knights of the Holy Sepulcher, which their founder had given them. After the ceremony, they ate together and talked.

The situation in the Pacific appeared favorable to Catholics in general and to the Picpuciens in particular. Gone were the days when a priest had been stabbed to death in the Tuamotus; when a bishop, seven priests, and ten sisters died as martyrs for Christ in the Marshalls; and when the Catholic missions were persecuted and expelled from Hawaii. On many isles now, chapels were going up, sometimes even fine big churches. The number of baptisms was growing daily. "The field has been plowed," declared the bishop. "Tomorrow we will gather in the harvest everywhere."

The eldest of the fathers raised his hand and shook his head, as if he had reservations.

"You don't agree, Fr. Raymond?" asked the prelate.

"You say 'everywhere,' Monsignor, but you have forgotten one island." All eyes turned toward Fr. Raymond, waiting for him to pronounce the name. "Molokai."

All brows darkened.

"Yes, Molokai," repeated Fr. Raymond. "The other islands are perhaps paradise, but Molokai is certainly hell. I have been there twice, and my eyes are still filled with the horror of what they saw. Yes, I know there are Catholics there. There is even a church. But there is no priest. We have withheld the consolation of Christ from those who need it most."

"I have often thought of Molokai," Msgr. Maigret said sadly, "but to send one of you, or all of you in rotation, to this hell — for you are right, Fr. Raymond, it is indeed a hell. I, too, have seen it. I have not been able to summon up the courage to do so."

"We are all ready to go to Molokai," said one of the missionaries.

"Some of my converts are there," said another. "I ask as a favor, Monsignor, to be allowed to join them in that island hell. The day of my solemn profession, did they not cover me with the black mantle of the dead, so that all might see that I was voluntarily giving up my life, the life of men? I am ready to be buried alive with those poor wretches."

The man who had just spoken was young, tall, with a fresh complexion and frank, intelligent eyes. He spoke with the slow, sing-song, slightly rasping voice that marked him as a lad from Flanders. He was in fact a Belgian, a Belgian from the lowlands, the son of a family of big Flemish farmers. The name on his birth certificate was Joseph de Veuster; his religious name, Fr. Damien.

Msgr. Maigret stared at Fr. Damien for a long moment, trying to make up his mind. Although still young, the Belgian was already an experienced missionary, with a record of outstanding success, not only in friendly districts like Puna, but among the thorny populations like Kohala. The bishop knew that the young Fleming had shown himself as courageous as he was capable, as vigorous as he was zealous, in the service of Christ. He had heard how one night during an earthquake, Fr. Damien had galloped on horseback after a poor Kanaka who, in a moment of panic, had slipped back into his old superstitions and was going to throw himself as a living sacrifice into the flaming maw of the volcano god. He had heard, too, how on his way to celebrate Mass in some out-of-the-way coastal village, the Belgian had wrecked his canoe on a coral reef during a storm and had swum ashore through shark-infested waters, but without losing the waterproof bag containing his portable altar. A lad like that was obviously fit for the terrible task under consideration.

"How old are you, Fr. Damien?" the bishop asked.

"Thirty-three."

"The age of our Lord at the moment of the Passion," said the bishop thoughtfully. After an instant of silence he asked: "Have you ever seen lepers, Father?"

"There's no lack of them at Kohala," the young priest replied with an angelic smile.

"If you have any hesitation about going to Molokai, I will understand perfectly," the bishop said. "I know you are attached to the faithful at your mission. . . . You stand by your offer? Good. Then go, in the name of the Lord."

Without a word, Fr. Damien knelt before the old bishop, whose episcopal ring flashed in the sunlight as he raised his hand in benediction.

∞

The little steamer Kilauea plowed through the sapphire waters of the strait, carrying a load of livestock from Oahu to Molokai. Standing at the rail, as mute and resigned as the cattle below decks, was a group of men, women, and children, staring straight ahead, apparently lost in deep despair. Many of them had swollen lips, distorted ears, or curious folds and nodules of flesh that transformed their faces into animal-like muzzles. Some had hands swathed in bandages. All had strange, dead complexions.

Two priests stood in the bow of the ship as on sentry duty. They did not speak. Msgr. Maigret prayed silently, his pale, old-man's lips moving slightly. Fr. Damien leaned his elbows on the railing, staring ahead like the lepers. The island rose slowly above the horizon, black and red. "Land of Precipices," the Kanakas called it, so torn and convulsed by volcanic upheavals was the island. Fr. Damien had never seen it before. He knew only that it was not like the other islands; that it was a sterile, rocky island, bristling with tufts of glossy grass and long-leafed cane. And he knew that the government leper colony was isolated on the Kalawao Peninsula, a promontory of some ten square miles, cut off from the rest of the island by the sheer cliff of the Pali — the worst spot on the island, people said, where a deep, wide crater lay like a gaping wound ever ready to pour forth its black blood of burning lava.

In the missionary's mind, souvenirs of childhood mingled with more recent impressions. He saw himself as a boy in Flanders, with his six brothers and sisters and the dear little white goat that pulled the cart he liked so much to ride in on Thursdays and Sundays. He saw again his little playmate Marieke in the plum-green dress she used to wear when she danced at the fair. He remembered well the day she had said to him with precocious solemnity: "I knew it, Jef. The good Lord has called you." He remembered, too, the day he had removed the bandages from an old Kanaka and found, instead of fingers, bleeding, stinking, suppurating stumps. And the sweet child he had treated in Kohala who had little by little been transformed by disease into a brown wooden skeleton with glassy eyes and claws for hands, and who had died at last of meningitis with a long, long cry, an animal cry that had lasted for hours.

And a fervent prayer arose from the soul of the priest: "Lord, was it not to give Your love to the most miserable of men that I left Trémeloo and the farm on which I was born, to go and knock on the door of the Fathers at Louvain? Was it not to testify for Thee and to carry Thy Word that I asked to be sent to the missions? Lord, I know the chalice that is being handed to me is filled with bitterness. Give me the strength to drink it, Lord, as Thou so gladly drank Thine own — to the dregs — to the end."

Molokai's black rocks were very close now. The people on the shore and the dock were waving. The little ship came alongside. The gangplank was made fast. The lepers went ashore, still silent, many in tears, setting foot for the first time on soil they would never leave. Some were greeted by friends or relatives who rushed forward with loud cries. There was heart-rending sobbing. Fr. Damien watched it all in stunned silence. These horrible faces, these animal snouts, these halt and lame, these maimed and pustular wrecks, these repulsive caricatures: this was the flock of which he would be shepherd!

"Lord, give me Thy strength," he murmured within him. "Lord, sustain me with Thy love! Lord, make me recognize Thy countenance in the face of each of these."

"Let's go ashore," said the gentle voice of Msgr. Maigret beside him.

The lepers had recognized the old bishop. They rushed toward him with arms outstretched, their eyes bright with joy. "Ka Ekopo! Ka Ekopo!" they cried. "Our bishop!" Some were kneeling, begging his benediction. Some limped toward the two priests. Still others ran into their huts to announce the news. Suddenly a group of lepers who were either drunk or mad, or both, rushed toward the two priests, screaming insults, curses, and threats. The others shut them up.

"I have come again to see you," said the bishop, "and this time, as you see, I have not come alone. Here is the man you have been waiting for. He will live among you now. He will be your father. He will take care of you. He will console you."

The lepers fell suddenly silent. They looked with astonishment at this handsome, husky, fair-haired man with the white skin who had come to live their life with them. An old man approached to examine Fr. Damien with an expert eye.

"You may inspect him," laughed the bishop. "He is perfectly healthy. Yet, as you see, he has come to live among you."

As he gestured toward the young missionary, the bishop noted that Fr. Damien was as white as a sheet. These faces, these tatters of humanity, the fierce cries of the drunken madmen, and especially, yes, especially the nauseating odor of decaying flesh which even the ocean breeze could not blow away . . . The bishop put his hand on the missionary's arm.

"Fr. Damien," he said in a low voice, "there is still time. The steamer does not start back for half an hour. If you wish, I will take you back with me. I will understand. There are some sacrifices that no man has the right to ask."

Fr. Damien looked the bishop squarely in the eyes. "I am staying, Monsignor," he said. "I am staying voluntarily. From now on, my life will have no other goal than to rebuild these pitiful creatures into men."

Then, turning to his new flock, he declared, "My children, I shall remain among you until I die. Your lives will be my life. Your bread will be my bread. And, if the good Lord wills it, your malady will one day be mine. I am ready to become a leper like you."

The steamer whistled as a signal for departure. The gangplank dropped. Standing in the stern, the old bishop raised his hands in blessing. For a long time, Fr. Damien stood watching the ship grow smaller as it headed back for Oahu. Then he started for his vicarage — a miserable hut of thatch next to the church. As he neared the hut, he heard a weak voice calling him. A man lay in a ditch, his eyes staring, his face a mass of sores. In one bound, the priest was beside him.

"What's the matter?" he asked.

"I'm hungry."

Fr. Damien fumbled in his bag. Thanks to God, he found a piece of bread he had not eaten. The blind leper devoured it ravenously.

"Why are you here?"

"The others put me out of my house, and I can no longer defend myself. They said I didn't need a house to die in."

A nameless horror gripped the heart of the priest. Molokai was indeed the last circle of hell. He raised the poor blind wretch and guided him to his hut next to the church. He put him to bed on the straw matting that was to have been his own. When he fell asleep, Fr. Damien went out into the night. It was a marvelous night, soft, warm, and gentle. In the darkness he could hear the throb of drums; the mad lepers were dancing about a fire, screaming.

"Lord, I place my soul in Thy hands," the missionary prayed. And he, too, fell asleep, completely exhausted, under a great pandanus tree on the fringe of the village. It was his first night among the Living Dead.

∞

Sixteen years! He was to spend sixteen years in this hell. The first years were atrocious. The destitution and misery of the district in which the lepers were isolated can scarcely be imagined. From time to time, the little boat brought enough provisions to keep the lepers from starving to death. But the outcasts were either too lazy or too listless to do anything to help themselves. Their farming was indifferent. Water was short in the colony, although there were abundant springs in the mountains. The shame of the colony was the hospital, which was an abomination. Everything was lacking. There were no doctors, no nurses, no medicines, not even any water. The hospital building itself was a fine stone structure covered with brightly colored flowers, but the patients inside were living corpses already eaten by worms.

Worst of all was the fact that these poor wretches, condemned to an awful death, instead of helping one another in a brotherly manner, behaved like wild beasts. One day Fr. Damien was walking past a long ditch that served as a dump for the colony when a man came along pushing a wheelbarrow, which he emptied into the ditch. At first, the missionary thought the man was throwing away a big bundle of rags, but the rags uttered a cry when they hit the dump — a dying leper. His fellow unfortunates had not even waited for his last breath before consigning him to the rubbish heap! Another time the Father was on his way to visit a dying man when he saw seven or eight lepers scurrying from the hut, all carrying heavy packages. Plunderers, too, were too impatient to wait for death.

Most men would have been discouraged by such abysmal suffering and iniquity. But Fr. Damien was a priest, a Catholic priest who had offered his life to the love of Christ. He did not flinch. As he had promised his bishop, he saw his duty clearly: to rebuild men from these ruins. Bravely he set to work.

The son of substantial Flemish farmers was no novice in the cultivation of land, and his arms were capable of the most rugged tasks. He undertook an extensive program of agriculture. He brought water from the mountain springs, at first by bucket brigades, which took off every morning, Fr. Damien in the lead, each man carrying two buckets. Then he planted crops wherever the soil was fertile. He launched a campaign of community sanitation. He burned down the worst of the disgusting old vermin-infested shacks and built new ones, the Father himself busily wielding hammer, saw, and trowel. He cleaned up the outskirts of the village. He laid out a cemetery, so the dead of the colony would no longer be dumped on the rubbish heap. It was a great day when the flume was finished, carrying pure spring water down the mountainside to the village. And it was an even greater day when the new church was completed and consecrated in a ceremony attended by every leper who could walk.

All the missionary's material labor was only the instrument of a greater work: evangelization. Or rather, in merely showing his true self, a wonderfully kind and charitable man who was constantly devoted to his leprous brothers, Fr. Damien was doing more for Christ than through a thousand sermons. His smiling face, his glad and comforting conversation, and the generosity of his heart won more souls than hours of preaching. The simple Kanakas recognized in him a true man of God. His conversions quickly multiplied; the number of baptisms increased. Many lepers who were still pagans learned the Gospel. Others, who had been baptized Protestants by Puritan missionaries who worked in the islands but never came near the leprosarium, were so impressed by seeing the priest living among them, helping them until their dying hour, that they became Catholics. A new climate of friendship and kindness was born on the peninsula of the Living Dead.

Fr. Damien used all means at his command to eliminate the causes of hate and misunderstanding. The drunkards were brought to their senses, and the distillation of alcohol, which had been going full blast when Fr. Damien arrived in Molokai, was forbidden. He guaranteed the police function himself. The wicked and the violent trembled in his presence. When he arrived on the scene of a free-for-all or an orgy, a billy in his fist, order was invariably restored with amazing promptness. The "evil good-for-nothings," as the missionary called them, would always decamp, pursued by the big stick of retribution.

Years passed. Fr. Damien's pleadings and protests finally attracted some attention to his dear lepers. Islanders began to talk about the extraordinary missionary who used the hammer, the saw, and the spade to win converts to Christ and the Gospel. The Honolulu newspapers printed articles about him. And the Kilauea brought shipments of beds, blankets, medicines, and provisions to Molokai. The nuns of Honolulu, who would themselves have loved to serve the lepers, collected money for the leprosarium and provided a new bell for the church there.

The publicity, which Fr. Damien had not sought and had even deplored, served him well in bringing essential help. But it had a bad side, too. It stirred up jealousy. The island authorities were not too happy to see one man do more for Molokai in a few years than they had accomplished in fifty. They began to make things difficult for him. The Protestant missionaries, who were still careful not to imitate Fr. Damien's example, were nevertheless furious at the many conversions he had made, and tried to bring pressure to bear. Efforts were made to get him out of Molokai. He refused to go. He received fine promises and impressive threats. He scorned them both. Finally he was attacked with a weapon that really hurt, despicable as it was. On the grounds that he might spread the infection to other islands, Fr. Damien was formally forbidden to leave the leprosarium for the rest of his life.

One day, when the *Kilauea* was approaching Molokai with its regular cargo of provisions and new lepers, Fr. Damien came alongside in a small boat and reached for the sea ladder. A Picpucien father was on board, a friend and superior of Fr. Damien.

"Push off!" cried the captain from the bridge. "Push off! I have received strict orders not to allow you on board."

"But I would like to speak to Fr. Modeste."

"My orders are that you are not to be allowed to speak to anyone whatever."

Crushed, on the verge of tears, Fr. Damien knelt in the small craft. "Father," he said, "hear my confession, I beg of you." And in a loud, clear voice, he confessed — in Latin.

Leaning over the ship's rail, his old superior, in tears, gave him absolution.

As the little ship disappeared behind the black cliffs, Fr. Damien returned to his church. His soul was torn, bleeding. But as he walked up the familiar road, he heard young, clear voices singing a hymn — the voices of his favorites, the children of the orphanage, his children, whom he had gathered in and raised, and taught to serve as altar boys at Mass. No, the wickedness of men would not defeat him! No, he would always remain *"Makua Kamiano,"* as the Kanakas called him. And, uniting his voice with those of the little lepers, he sang a hymn to the Holy Virgin, Our Lady of Consolation.

∞

Early in December of 1884 — he had been on Molokai for nearly twelve years — Fr. Damien returned home from a long hard horseback ride in the mountains, during which he had been caught in a violent tropical rainstorm. As he dismounted, he called to his housekeeper (a leper, of course, but not far advanced), "Mother Anna, please heat some water for a good footbath. I'm soaked to the skin and as cold as an icicle."

A quarter of an hour later, the good woman brought the steaming tub with the caution "Take care, Makua Kamiano. The water is boiling hot. Don't burn yourself."

Fr. Damien carefully tested the water with a tip of one big toe. No, it wasn't too hot. He put both feet into the tub.

Mother Anna watched him, first with amazement, then with anguish. She knew what was happening.

"Curious," said Fr. Damien. "Your water is steaming, yet my feet still feel cold."

The missionary lifted one foot and examined it. He gave a little cry. The skin of the foot was red and blistered! Then he, too, understood. One of the first symptoms of leprosy, after months, even years of incubation, is the disappearance of surface sensitivity. The skin no longer feels — neither hot nor cold, nor the prick of a pin — nothing!

Leprosy! So Fr. Damien had become a leper! He stood up and walked to the little mirror that was his dressing aid. He examined his reflection at length. He could see no signs of the malady in his face as yet, nor on his hands. He also inspected his body. He could find no nodules, no scaly areas of discoloration of the skin. But he was under no illusions. The terrible malady, against which no remedy had as yet been efficacious, would follow its normal course. Perhaps the new injections he had heard about would delay its advance. But little by little it would take over his entire body. His face, his nose, his eyes . . .

A great and human sadness overwhelmed him. But his priestly conscience was far stronger than his reactions to the disintegration of his sense of feeling. Had he not sacrificed everything to Christ, even his life? Had he not pledged aloud to his parishioners on his arrival at Molokai that he was ready to become a leper if such should be the will of God? Well, the hour had come, and he was indeed ready. Kneeling before his little crucifix, he murmured, "Thy will be done, Lord, and not mine."

It would take him four years to die. The disease was almost merciful to him, inasmuch as it left his eyes until the last, and spared him the abominable purulent decay of his limbs which he had seen in so many other lepers. But his face, the handsome face of the honest Flemish peasant, grew swollen, deformed, and burgeoning with nodules. The husky, healthy lad who had landed sixteen years ago on the Isle of the Living Dead was no longer recognizable.

And yet, as he neared the end of his term, Fr. Damien became a celebrity. Little by little, the fame of this extraordinary man spread throughout the world. Every boat brought newspapers from Europe and America, all of them carrying laudatory (and somewhat awed) articles about the man a Belgian journalist called "the hero of Molokai." A French newspaper called him "the apostle to the lepers." A German daily headlined its piece, "You who pass before the cliffs of Molokai, bow low." If they thought he would be pleased by this fulsome praise, they were mistaken. He was annoyed. It was not for cheap publicity that he had exiled himself to the ends of the earth. He would have greatly preferred to remain unknown to all, except the Lord.

But the unwanted publicity did help Fr. Damien. His enemies were disarmed. The jealous dared not act overtly. The administration was forced by public opinion to grant a more generous budget to the colony. Princess Liliuokalani, later Queen of Hawaii, paid a visit to the leprosarium, admired the work of Fr. Damien, and awarded him a high decoration. Money and gifts came from all over. A new medicine invented by a Japanese doctor was sent to Molokai in an effort to save the heroic missionary's life. But Fr. Damien had no false hopes. He knew the moment was near when the Lord would call him to His side.

He had only one worry: would his work disappear with him? He was soon reassured that it would continue. Helpers were coming to Molokai. An American officer arrived to join his service, followed by a Belgian priest who had been his friend in college. Several nuns landed on the island to care for the orphans. His own brother, who had become a Picpucien, spoke of coming to join him. The seed that Fr. Damien had planted in the barren soil of Molokai had taken root and would continue to grow after his death. He could go away happy.

He continued working to the last. In his dying months, he started to build a new church for the future. The last weeks were extremely painful. The lesions had grown more numerous and more frightful. Although suffering greatly, he refused the bed his friends had prepared for him. He had to be put there by force. His last instructions were for the distribution of his few poor personal belongings and the dollars and pounds sterling that had come to him from the four corners of the world.

He died peacefully on April 15, 1889. According to his wishes, he was buried under the big pandanus outside the village, the very tree under which he slept his first night among the Living Dead.

Fr. Nussbaum

∞

Martyr of the Forbidden Tibet

The great missionary adventure is not finished, nor will it ever be until the end of time. "Go ye, therefore, and make disciples of all the nations,"[25] was the Master's last order; and there will always be Christians with the faith, the courage, and the spirit of enterprise to carry it out. The task still to be accomplished is immense. Although it is true that Christianity today may count 500,000,000 baptized souls, there are still a billion and a half who have never heard the message, who know nothing whatever of the word of God. It is to these men and women still deep in the shadows that thousands of missionaries are devoting themselves. By the Word, by the testimony of their lives, and even more by their inexhaustible charity, these men and women of God are carrying the Gospel to the far corners of the world, preparing new Christendoms for tomorrow.

No, the breed of God's Adventurers is not extinct. On the contrary, their number has grown considerably in recent years.

[25] Matt. 28:19.

And there is no great order that does not have a branch dedicated to this work. There are Jesuit missionaries, just as there are Franciscan missionaries. The Trappists, like the Benedictines, have convents in far countries to demonstrate Christian piety to the Buddhists of Asia and the souls in Africa. And let us not forget the women's orders, the sisters of charity and the teaching sisters, who in the four corners of the earth give to the Christ the testimony of their limitless charity.

Thus, in our day, men and women for the love of the Lord are still undertaking adventures every bit as thrilling as those of St. Paul, Bl. Ramon Lull, or Fr. de Foucauld. There are still in our day missionaries like Fr. Damien among the lepers. There are missionaries living, in the jungles of Africa, much the same kind of life that St. Isaac Jogues once lived among the Indians.

New technical means now at man's disposition have allowed the apostles of Christ to widen their field of action without lessening the dangers. Thus, the oblate missionaries in the deserts of the Great North who serve Canadian and Alaskan parishes as big as a quarter of France risk their lives daily by flying in subzero temperatures, through black fogs and blizzards. And human malice continues to oppose the spokesmen of the Good News. The peril of death comes from men as well as from nature. Today, unknown heroes die so that the Gospel may be carried to the ends of the earth. The time of the missionary martyrs has not yet passed.

And here is one of them, still almost unknown, who would doubtless have been greatly surprised to hear himself cited as an example, for in his deep humility, he thought he was doing no more than his simple duty in the service of the Master. He died only after the beginning of World War II.

∞

Tibet is a country in the heart of Asia with an area four times as great as that of France. It consists mostly of a plateau nearly three miles above sea level, crossed by mountain chains that are two miles higher. Its climate is frightful — polar because of the altitude and desert-like because it lies in the zone of the rainless steppes. Even in summer, the temperature often drops to freezing, and in winter frequently goes to 30 degrees below zero Fahrenheit and colder. On the other hand, as the summer sun beats down, the thermometer climbs well above 100 degrees. The Tibetans wear furs the year round and smear their faces with grease or wrap them in cloth to keep their skin from cracking. Only the valley bottoms are fertile. The natives grow some barley there and raise long-horned sheep and yaks. The yak, a very shaggy animal resembling a buffalo, is the true wealth of this poor country and serves as a beast of burden as well as a source of milk and meat.

It is not surprising that men living in such a hostile environment — and there are not many of them — should live in constant difficulty, in mediocrity, and in error. When Buddhism became the religion of Tibet, it was mingled with a residue of superstition that had gripped the country from time immemorial. The Tibetan is constantly surrounded by devils, evil forces, and dangerous spirits. He himself calls his country the Land of Spirits. The dead are supposed to come back to threaten the living. Many crimes and mysterious disappearances are explained by stories of strange magic. There are, of course, pure, sincerely religious men among the lamas who live in the great Buddhist monasteries; but the majority of the Buddhist clergy are mediocre folk, quite as steeped in superstition as the rest of the people. What miserable soil in which to sow the Gospel of Christ!

The Church, however, considered this sterile ground no more desperate than any other. If a few rare missionaries could penetrate into the heart of Tibet on journeys of exploration, it would perhaps be possible to plant a few signposts that would mark the road to be followed later. Most easily accessible was the east — Chinese Tibet, theoretically under the rule of Peking, but actually almost independent. The plateau did not extend very far in that direction. Instead the countryside was marked with splendid mountains and deep valleys through which ran the upper reaches of the majestic rivers of China, Burma, and Indo-China: the Yangtze, the Mekong, and the Salween. The lower regions are less than four thousand feet high, and the mountain passes stand at ten thousand to fifteen thousand feet.

By European standards, this saw-tooth country seems well-nigh impenetrable; by Tibetan standards, it seems quite accessible. Thus, the door to Asia, the "Tea Route" followed by caravans for thousands of years, passed this way. By this way also did the Church of Christ undertake her assault on the heart of Asia.

The missionaries began to drift into Chinese Tibet toward the end of the nineteenth century. In 1910, the Pope created the Vicariate Apostolic of Kien-chang, which today is an administration headed by a titular bishop. The first Vicar Apostolic for this Tibetan district was Msgr. de Guébriant, a man of exceptional valor, and a great apostle. Under his energetic impetus, the mission posts multiplied. The pioneers of Christ who manned them were members of the Paris Society of Foreign Missions, a great organization that has been increasing its efforts and sacrifices throughout the Far East since the seventeenth century, seeking especially to create a native priesthood to work among their blood brothers. The "Missionaries of the Rue du Bac," as they are called in Paris, have done inestimable good in India, China, Japan, Manchuria, and Korea.

In 1931, the mission post of Sido-weisi on the upper reaches of the Mekong was confided to Fr. Nussbaum, an old backwoodsman and pioneer of Christ, old not in years but in his extraordinary experience in a region infested with brigands, both Lolo and Tibetan. Fr. Nussbaum was no older than fifty, but he had spent twenty-three years in this wild country. He was a little man but a husky one, with nerves and muscles of steel tempered by his mission years. His calm, unwrinkled face was framed with a long, blond beard. He had light blue eyes, always gentle. His most striking traits were his eternal good humor, his quiet courage, and his trust in Providence. For more than twenty years, he had risked his life daily in this mission at the ends of the earth just as calmly as if he were parish priest in some sleepy village of his native Alsace. He had once and for all sacrificed his everything to the Lord: his happiness, his comfort, his life. Why should he start worrying about it now?

Heroes of God

The mission in this lost valley of Tibet had some of the external characteristics of a fortress. Backed against the ramparts of the little town, the mission formed a separate enclosure surrounded by a crenelated wall as a precaution against an always-possible attack. Several buildings stood inside the wall: the chapel, the missionary's residence, and a combination stable and storehouse. The setting was wildly beautiful: high, reddish cliffs dominated by snowcapped peaks surrounding the plain, through which the river flowed in a deep gorge. A little rice grew in the valley and much barley; but the town depended on the caravans that stopped there on their way to and from Upper Tibet.

Fr. Nussbaum was almost a Tibetan himself after so many years in the country. He spoke the languages fluently — not only Tibetan, but Chinese and the crude dialect of the Lolos; so he could express himself easily to all comers, which is, after all, the first duty of a missionary. His clothing was a picturesque compromise between the cassock, which he raised with a belt, and the Tibetan garb, of which he had adopted the soft leather boots and even the furs. He lived in complete Tibetan style, which took some effort at the beginning, for Tibetan cuisine is not something that would appeal to a European gourmet. The principal dish was a stew of barley and chickpeas in which was cooked — if it would cook — some sort of pickled meat which, if it was not spoiled, was apt to be as hard as wood. This was washed down with a bowl of bitter, salty tea in which had been melted a chunk of butter as rancid as possible. He slept on a wooden panel covered with stiff, thick bedclothes, which bore little resemblance to any bed he had seen at home.

His physical discomforts, however, seemed unimportant compared with his other troubles. He got used to hearing himself called *Yang Kwee-tze* several times a day, for all Europeans were classified as "foreign devils." But he had to be on constant guard against the intrigues of the lamas. Religious hatred drove the Buddhist priests to eternal agitation against the missionary, several times reaching the point of abetting attempted murder. And when, after much time and effort, he had won some good soul to the Gospel, he had to be ever watchful to keep him from backsliding into his old superstitions, his idolatrous cults, his magic rites, or simply his old drunken habits. All this effort, all this tenacity, all this obscure heroism so that a few hundred Asian men, women, and children might know the Truth of God and the Word of Christ!

But this was nothing new. For a missionary, a smashing success is not nearly so important as giving his testimony and trusting in the Lord for the rest. So Fr. Nussbaum, his bright blue eyes sparkling as gaily as a child's, was able to laugh quietly in the midst of his worst difficulties.

∞

Early in 1931, the region of the Upper Mekong was agog over the arrival of a little caravan with big plans. The idea had been long taking shape in the mind of Msgr. de Guébriant — since 1918, in fact, when he was caught in a snowstorm during an inspection trip through the Tibetan mountains. At that time, the Vicar Apostolic of Kien-chang thought of the admirable hospices in the Alpine passes, where sturdy, tireless men stood ever ready to help the traveler in trouble. Those known to the public as the Fathers of the Great St. Bernard, but who are actually the regular canons of Martigny-en-Valais, were carrying on a remarkable work of charity, with the aid of their famous dogs — saving human lives at the price of their own, helping the injured, carrying down the dead whom the mountain had killed. The mountain passes of Tibet were even more treacherous than those of the Alps. There were no roads without their quota of human skeletons, blanched by wind and cold, of travelers surprised by a storm, buried by snow, or murdered by brigands.

"What we need here," the great missionary bishop had said to himself, "would be hospices conceived in the same spirit as those of Grand St. Bernard and other mountain passes in Europe where travelers may find shelter. What a blessing they would be! What a beneficent influence our men of God could have on those whom they would save, protect, and care for!"

When the provost first proposed his idea to the canons of the Grand St. Bernard, it did not take them long to adopt it enthusiastically. The mountains of Europe had been partially tamed by tunnels, the automobile, snowplows, and the airplane. In Asia, however, the Fathers of St. Bernard would find a new opportunity to practice their original vocation. When their superior asked for volunteers, many hands were raised. But only two were chosen for a first voyage of reconnaissance.

In the latter days of November 1930, two young priests, Canons Melly and Goquoz, sailed from Marseilles for the Far East to explore the possibility of establishing at some mountain pass along the Tea Route a hospice in the tradition of St. Bernard. Although the priests were in perfect condition and trained in many sports, the journey they were called upon to make was not exactly a vacation. Landing at Hanoï in Indo-China, they traveled by rail to Yünnanfu. Then they started to walk — a little walk of 1,500 miles, about the distance from Paris to the Caspian Sea — through unknown country, over almost trackless land at times, constantly on the watch for brigands and for hotheads stirred up by anti-foreign agitators and by anti-Christian lamas who, once they had heard of the new project, set out to block it. For the young missionaries, their first foreign assignment was a grueling cross-country contest.

When, after many adventures, the two priests reached the Chinese city of Ningyenfu, which had just fallen into the hands of Communist generals fighting the Chiang Kai-shek government, they were surprised to be greeted by a missionary with a fine, blond beard who held out his arms and laughed. Fr. Nussbaum, having been notified by Msgr. de Guébriant of the impending arrival of the young men from Switzerland, had simply walked over three hundred miles of mountain trails to greet them and act as their guide. It was a valuable service. His knowledge of the language and customs of the country warded off many troubles that the young men could have experienced, such as going astray or being ambushed by bandits.

Despite the magic presence of Fr. Nussbaum, the rest of the journey of the two priests was a novel of adventure. The athletic training of the young Swiss and the calm competence of Fr. Nussbaum could not avert the normal risks of the road. The three priests with their guides and mules and servants followed the same rocky trail that had been in use since the Middle

Ages. Crossing streams was a particular problem. The men were sometimes loaded into a rickety ferry, usually an antique junk that, despite the efforts of the paddlers and their rhythmic shouts, would be carried a mile downstream by the current, with the animals swimming behind at the end of a towline. Sometimes they crossed on a so-called bridge, an affair of three ropes of woven bamboo stretched over roaring waters, the upper two ropes serving as guard rails, the third as a walkway. Sometimes there was only one bamboo rope, which they had to cross by gripping a pulley that slid over the foaming current along the rope. One of these crossings almost cost Fr. Nussbaum his life. He and his horse fell when a precarious bridge collapsed, and they were dashed against the rocks by the swift current.

At night, the trio had to cope with bedbugs, mosquitoes, beetles, and cockroaches, or a few serpents that made their way into the sleeping quarters. Every gorge they crossed was a challenge to the local brigands. One such ravine was called "The Vale of Death" and apparently had earned its nickname. One village at which they stopped for the night was attacked and burned to the terrifying accompaniment of screams and gunfire.

None of this had the slightest cooling effect on the zeal of the fathers. They did not slow their advance. In turn, they crossed the Yangtze and the Mekong. They crossed a pass more than two miles high and came in sight of the Salween — and their goal. For it was in the Latsa Pass that Fr. Nussbaum advised the young men to establish their haven. Latsa, at an altitude of some twelve thousand feet, was on a well-traveled caravan route. More than thirty thousand porters trudged through the pass every year. It was an ideal location in which to carry on their charity. The two Swiss priests surveyed the site carefully, made note of everything they would need to make the installation a safe one, then started back for the Grand St. Bernard to report to their superiors. The creation of a hospice at Latsa Pass was approved.

∞

Work began at Latsa four years later, in the summer of 1935. Trees were felled in the middle of a great circle of majestic rocks. There was a fine spring nearby to guarantee the water supply. With the aid of two laymen who had returned with the Swiss canons to share their risks and efforts, and helped by native workers, the two fathers quickly laid the foundation for the hospice. The white foreign devils soon became the talk of the region. They were mad, of course, to want to build in this isolated spot, in this hostile pass where nobody in his right mind would dream of living, let alone establishing a monastery. But the Buddhist priests in every lamasery in the region regarded the enterprise, not only with suspicion, but with growing hate.

While waiting for the haven to become livable, the Swiss priests bedded down at Sido-weisi and, instead of marking time, worked hard for the Faith. They founded a sort of seminary in which they taught some of the local children the rudiments of European civilization and even a little Latin, hoping to lead some of them to the priesthood. Some adults were converted. A second group of Swiss canons arrived on the Upper

Mekong in July 1936, and the missionary activity was increased by the arrival of reinforcements. So was the angry distrust of the lamas.

Fr. Nussbaum, however, was no longer on the scene. Now that his dear valley of the Mekong had been invaded by so many men of God capable of carrying to fruition the work he had started, he must consider his task as one of God's pioneers completed in this area. He must push on further, where there was still trouble and danger to be overcome.

Beyond Chinese Tibet to the North lay the boundaries of Forbidden Tibet, so called because since 1745, the country had been closed to Europeans and, it goes without saying, particularly priests. This was the land of the Dalai Lama, "the Living Buddha," the grand priest of the lamas and the reincarnation of Buddha himself. If the lamas of Chinese Tibet had looked with great suspicion upon the activities of the Christian missionaries, those of Forbidden Tibet would stop at nothing to block this foreign influence. This is actually what tempted the good, gentle Fr. Nussbaum.

His plan was simple. He would abandon his residence at Sido-weisi to the canons of St. Bernard, who would thus be in constant communication with the hospice in the pass. He himself would go on to Yerkalo in Forbidden Tibet to work on spreading the Gospel. Not far from Yerkalo was the Lamasery of Karmda whose Chief Lama was reported to be a cruel and violent man, the sworn enemy of any Christian priest.

Nothing could deter Fr. Nussbaum from trying his experiment. His superiors granted the necessary authorization. Fr. Tornay, a brave canon of St. Bernard, asked permission to accompany him. The two Catholic priests thus found themselves in the very midst of a hostile population, within sight of the walls of the enemy lamasery, so close they could hear the constant tolling of the bells and the whirr of the prayer wheels. Curiously enough, this bold move succeeded admirably. Not only did the impressive courage of the two men forestall any hostile action, but the people of the village seemed relatively responsive to Christianity. In three years, the two priests baptized 350 Tibetans. A Christian tree seemed to be taking root and growing in the very heart of Lamaist Tibet.

And yet Fr. Nussbaum was under no illusion. Like all great missionaries, he was thinking of martyrdom. He accepted it in advance and even, deep in his great Christian heart, hoped for it. He remembered all those who before him had wet this hostile soil with their blood. He thought of Fr. Mussot, who, on April 6, 1905, was attacked by a mob incited by the lamas, stripped of his clothes, beaten until he bled, then shot to death point blank. He thought of Fr. Soulié, who, a week later, was shot through the head and through the heart, and then decapitated so that the mob could use his head for a football. He thought, too, of the Christian natives of this very Yerkalo, the converts of Fr. Mussot and Fr. Soulié, who, four days later, on April 18, had been massacred to the last man, woman, and child. He thought of Fr. Bourdonne, bristling with arrows like St. Sebastian;[26] of Fr. Dubernard, whose torture had lasted two days, dragged barefoot for miles, mocked and sneered at for

---

[26] St. Sebastian (d. 304), Christian Roman soldier who was martyred under Diocletian.

hours and hours by the lamas, who suggested that he adopt their faith and finally had him decapitated by an executioner so clumsy that it took three sword strokes to sever his head. The last on the list of martyrs in Tibet was Fr. Monbeig, ambushed and shot in a mountain gorge. The last? Or would Fr. Nussbaum himself be the last?

The fury of the Grand Lama of Karmda grew with each new Christian convert. He had just sent a delegation to the Dalai Lama in Lhasa, urging him to expel every Occidental priest in Tibet, those in Yerkalo as well as those at Latsa Pass, when the second World War broke out. The hospice was already two stories high, and the two missionaries at Yerkalo were winning more souls to Christ every day. When the news from Europe reached this distant land, there was great rejoicing among the lamas. The Japanese advance into Yünnan would soon isolate the Christians on the Upper Mekong, leaving them to the ill will of the lamas.

Communication with Europe being for all practical purposes cut off, the missionaries were in a desperate situation that lasted for years. They sold their poor belongings, even their clothing, in an attempt to maintain their groups of young Christians. Lack of money halted construction of the hospice, and the half-finished walls were soon crumbling under the impact of high winds and driving snow.

The people themselves, however, showed no hostility to the priests. Their limitless kindness had won many hearts, and their care and medicines had been a godsend to the sick. Some of the young Christians went into business to help support the missionaries. Months passed.

The Grand Lama of Karmda had bided his time. His envoys to the Dalai Lama had not returned, perhaps the victims
of bandits or the weather. Now he decided to take advantage
of the circumstances and act on his own. Rather than soil his
own hands with blood, even European blood, he took counsel
with a bandit chief named Tchrachi, well known in the region
for his countless misdeeds. The head of a gang of footloose
men who lived by holding up caravans, pillaging villages, and
plundering at random, he seemed immune from control or
punishment. The Chinese officer commanding the little post
at Sido-weisi learned this to his sorrow. When he tried to put a
stop to the gang's activities, the bandit chief kidnapped and
killed the officer's son. The gang leader's morals were worthy
of the blackest days of the Middle Ages. He profited by the
chaotic state of the country, which was not sure whether it was
under Chinese or Japanese control — or was it the Communist generals who were running things?

The great enemy of the Lama of Karmda was Fr. Nussbaum,
whose very presence in Forbidden Tibet was a crime in the
eyes of the theocrat. Moreover, he was more vulnerable than
the other priests, who lived in groups. Fr. Nussbaum was almost always alone. And yet even the lonely missionary of
Yerkalo was not easy to dispose of. To attack him in the village
itself would be risking a battle with his native Christian converts. He would have to be closely watched during one of his
frequent journeys to visit a colleague or to carry the Word of
God to some distant group of Tibetan Christians.

Early in September 1941, Fr. Nussbaum left to go into retreat at Tse-chung, where his superior, Fr. Goré, and his friend

Fr. Lovey were stationed. He left Canon Tornay in charge of the mission at Yerkalo. On the way out he was indeed ambushed and surrounded by bandits. They were not the terrible Tchrachi's men, however, but of a lesser breed, and the missionary was able to bribe his way to freedom.

The return trip was a different story. Fr. Nussbaum's little caravan consisted of a bearer and three Tibetan Catholic girls who were going to Yerkalo with him to teach catechism. The first two stages of the journey were without incident. At the end of the third day, however, the missionary sensed danger in the air.

The travelers reached Napu, a little village at the start of the long, steep climb to the pass leading to Yerkalo, intending to spend the night there. When the villagers refused shelter to the Christians, however, they pushed on. Several lamas they passed on the road eyed them with hate. Then, as they started the climb, a friendly woman whom they met warned Fr. Nussbaum that Tchrachi lay in ambush at the pass.

The little caravan returned to Napu, where every door was still locked against them. They camped in the village marketplace — but not for long. The mice would not come to the cat? Then the cat would come to the mice.

The darkness was filled with bandit yells and the terrified screams of the three Tibetan maidens. Then came threats, arguments, and the usual bargaining for ransom. The brigand chief demanded three hundred piasters. Fr. Nussbaum offered thirty. They compromised on thirty pieces of silver, plus all the tea in the caravan and two blankets.

The three weeping maidens could not believe they were free to proceed. They thanked God for having delivered them. And the Christian caravan moved on to Pamé.

At Pamé, they had reason to believe themselves safe. The mission there was solidly built and fortified. There was food, and they could rest. The night was warm, so the bearer and the three girls slept outside on the terrace. Fr. Nussbaum retired to his room to read his breviary.

During the night, six armed men climbed to the terrace. Awakening with a start, neither the bearer nor the girls had time to cry out. At gun's point, they were forced from bed and their hands tied behind them.

The bandits then battered down Fr. Nussbaum's door, tied his hands, and bound him to a post. The moment he had been expecting, the moment of martyrdom, had come at last.

But the bandits were in no hurry. First they sacked the mission, stealing everything they could carry off, eating and drinking their fill. Then they marched their prisoners out of the village while the terrified villagers, even the Christians among them, stood by helplessly.

Fr. Nussbaum was without shoes. The rocky path tore his socks to shreds and drew blood from his feet. Where were they taking him? Wasn't this the path leading down to the stream, to the deserted mill? Wherever the path led, the missionary knew that God would be waiting for him at the end. He could not delude himself. The brigand walking behind him held the muzzle of a gun pressed between his shoulder blades.

Fr. Nussbaum staggered a little, as the stones bit painfully into his feet. He prayed as he walked, raising his eyes to the stars from time to time. When they reached the edge of the ravine and the path started down steeply toward the stream, the man behind the missionary pulled the trigger. One shot was enough. The bullet pierced the priest's heart. Fr. Nussbaum fell dead.

One after the other, the bandits stepped up to peer at the body of the dead priest. Then they set the four other prisoners free. Their job concerned only Fr. Nussbaum. They had done their work. They disappeared into the night.

At daybreak the diabolic clangor of gongs and bells at the Lamasery of Karmda proclaimed victory for the Grand Lama, while a little group of Christians from Pamé walked sadly to the edge of the ravine to recover the saintly remains of a man of God. The Church could count one more martyr. A new name had been added to the honor roll of God's Adventurers, the name of a hero.

Henri Daniel-Rops

(1901-1965)

The much-beloved Catholic historian and author Henri Daniel-Rops was born Henri Jules Charles Petiot in France in 1901. The grandson of peasants and the son of an artillery officer, he showed early in life the brilliance and intellectual dynamism that would bring him worldwide renown as a writer: Before he was twenty-one, he had earned the equivalent of Master's degrees in law, geography, and history.

He became a teacher, but quickly showed that his first love — and his greatest talent — was writing. His first book, *Our Anxiety,* was published in 1926 under the *nom de plume* Henri Daniel-Rops, which he continued to use to the end of his life.

By this time Daniel-Rops, raised a Catholic, had fallen away from the Church and become an agnostic. *Our Anxiety* reflects his spiritual restlessness. By the 1930s, however, he had made his way back to the Catholic Faith. He found, according to his biographer Justine Krug Buisson, that "only in

Jesus Christ could the technological age be reconciled with the spiritual needs of man."

Already an accomplished historian, Daniel-Rops became fascinated by the workings of God in history. His writings began to reflect this preoccupation. He wrote a history of the Jews before Christ (*Sacred History*), an account of the apostolic Church (*The Church of Apostles and Martyrs*), and a *History of the Church of Christ*. Many regard his book *Jesus and His Times* as his greatest achievement. It was a huge bestseller in France, catapulting this energetic historian to worldwide renown and winning his books attention, not only from Catholics, but from many non-Catholics as well.

In addition to teaching, lecturing, and writing, Daniel-Rops was director of the French publishing house Fayard, as well as the popular French religious magazine *Ecclesia*. He still found the time to write more than seventy books: novels, historical studies, poetry, and children's stories. He was also editor-in-chief of the massive 150-volume *Twentieth-Century Encyclopedia of Catholicism*.

His writings brought him many honors. He was elected to the French Academy in 1955, in which he became the youngest member. The following year, Pope Pius XII awarded him the Cross of the Order of St. Gregory the Great. He was greatly respected for his ability to express ancient spiritual truths with a new freshness and a journalistic sense of immediacy. His strong Catholic faith allows readers to draw from each of his works, not only the historical context of the great events of the Church, but also a fervent reaffirmation of the love and Providence of God.

∞

Sophia Institute Press®

Sophia Institute™ is a nonprofit institution that seeks to restore man's knowledge of eternal truth, including man's knowledge of his own nature, his relation to other persons, and his relation to God. Sophia Institute Press® serves this end in numerous ways: it publishes translations of foreign works to make them accessible to English-speaking readers; it brings out-of-print books back into print; and it publishes important new books that fulfill the ideals of Sophia Institute™. These books afford readers a rich source of the enduring wisdom of mankind. Sophia Institute Press® makes these high-quality books available to the general public by using advanced technology and by soliciting donations to subsidize its general publishing costs. Your generosity can help Sophia Institute Press® to provide the public with editions of works containing the enduring wisdom of the ages. Please send your tax-deductible contribution to the address below.

For your free catalog, call:
Toll-free: 1-800-888-9344

Sophia Institute Press® ◆ Box 5284 ◆ Manchester, NH 03108
www.sophiainstitute.com

Sophia Institute™ is a tax-exempt institution as defined by the
Internal Revenue Code, Section 501(c)(3). Tax I.D. 22-2548708.